RO
ROTTERS
AND C

ROGUES, ROTTERS, RASCALS AND CHEATS

The Greatest Sporting Scandals

JOHN PERRY

JOHN BLAKE

Published by John Blake Publishing Ltd,
3 Bramber Court, 2 Bramber Road,
London W14 9PB, England

www.blake.co.uk

First published in paperback in 2007

ISBN: 978 1 84454 468 4

British Library Cataloguing-in-Publication Data:

A catalogue record for this book is available from the British Library.

Design by www.envydesign.co.uk

Printed in Great Britain by CPI Bookmarque, Croydon, CR0 4TD

1 3 5 7 9 10 8 6 4 2

Papers used by John Blake Publishing are natural, recyclable products
made from wood grown in sustainable forests. The manufacturing processes
conform to the environmental regulations of the country of origin.

Every attempt has been made to contact the relevant copyright-holders,
but some were unobtainable. We would be grateful if the appropriate
people could contact us.

For Jack, who would never cheat

Acknowledgements

Many thanks to Daniel Kennett, of the *Sun*'s sports picture desk, for researching the pictures in this book, and to the staff of the News International reference library in Wapping.

Contents

Foreword   XIII

1   Brass Necks

Marathon by Motor   1
Bloody Nerve   6
Just Not Cricket   10
Goalflinger   15
Marathon by Rail   17
The Hand of God   18
The Fast and the Furious   22
Race from the Finish   27
Dive of the Century   29

2   Nobblers

The Felling of the All Blacks   35
Ice Scream   38
The £10 Million Tummy Bug   44

3 Fixers

Guided by Satan   47
India's Mr Fixit   59
Captain Crook   62
Mockery of a Match   66
Ballpark Figures   69
Black Wednesday   79
The Great Bungs Battle   83
Dim Sums   86
Serie A's Business   89

4 Druggies

Suspect Device   95
King of Cheats   98
Deceit of a Nation   109
Laboratory Rats   113
Speed Freak   116
Drug Pedaller   120
Deep Trouble   124

5 Imposters

Fit as a Fiddle   129
Hidden Agender   134
Blade Runner   136
The Painted Horse   137
Dia, Oh Dia, Oh Dia   141
Little Big Man   145
Herman the German   149
He Ain't Heavy   150
The Woman Who Wasn't   154
Nagging Suspicion   155

6 Fiddlers

Tamper, Tamper	159
Foiled Again	165
Corking Excuse	169
A Bat Out of Hell	171

7 Tricksters

The Dubious Hat	173
No Winnings, No Cry	175
Faker in the Fog	176
Water Mitty	178
Ears What We'll Do	182
The Bogus Race Meeting	184
King-Sized Hoax	186
Shove Off	189

8 Rotters

The Referee's a Banker	191
Robbed Roy	194
Golden Fleeced	196

9 Sneaks

Underhand Tactics	199
Unholey Stink	203
Admission of Defeet	205

10 A Cheat? Not Me!

Dirt in the Pocket	209
Toiletgate	214
Bodyline	216

Foreword

Cheating is as old as sport. We're all born with the dark desire to gain unfair advantage over our opponents. Some of us can't resist it. It follows, therefore, that even in the very first sporting events – the recreational archery depicted in Neolithic paintings – some crafty cave dweller will have used an illicitly whittled bow or illegally flighted arrows. He may also have been pumped up and buzzing from unauthorised extra rations of raw meat. Maybe he simply lied about where his arrows landed.

Even the ancient gods were at it. Greek myth contains the story of Atalanta, the world's fastest woman, who consented to marry a suitor named Melanion only if he could outrun her. Melanion had no chance. But Aphrodite, goddess of love, came to his aid, handing him three golden apples, which one by one he proceeded to drop during the race. Atalanta could not resist stopping to retrieve them and Melanion stormed to victory, winning her hand in the process. Who says cheats never prosper?

This book doesn't set out to examine the ethics of cheating. I could discuss how the explosion of diving in football is cheating opponents out of a fair game and the paying public out of a contest of skill. I could talk about how our great joy at witnessing some Herculean feat of athletics is wrenched from us once the hero is revealed to have been chemically assisted. I could examine how the prevalence of drugs in a major event like, say, the Tour de France undermines its very existence. I could talk about how the colossal rewards of sporting success in the 21st century have made cheating inevitable – if you can't beat 'em, you'd better join 'em.

But I'll leave all that to others far more qualified to write about it. This book simply asks you to put your indignation aside and enjoy the greatest tales in the long, ignoble history of cheating in sport. Some date from more innocent times, where the aim was merely to gain an advantage, perhaps a medal. Others are shameful, criminal efforts to con the hapless punter. I have tried to celebrate the cunning and audacity of some scoundrels, while highlighting the shameless villainy and rank stupidity of others.

In pursuit of the most complete tome possible, I have even covered a handful of characters who were *not* cheats. This may seem like cheating on my part, so let me explain. I have included them, despite their innocence, because they caused great cheating controversies. England's 'Bodyline' bowlers, for instance, triggered the greatest scandal in cricket's history, but they were not cheats. Unless you are Australian.

John Perry

Chapter 1

Brass Necks

MARATHON BY MOTOR
Fred Lorz

Fred Lorz would surely have a claim to a gold medal for the greatest cheat in Olympic history if such a dubious honour existed, for Lorz won the 1904 marathon thanks to a ten-mile car ride.

Lorz's illicit recovery from exhaustion in the back of his manager's motor is just one episode in a hilariously shambolic race that typified the chaotic Games held in St Louis. As the Olympic historian David Wallechinksy said, 'It ranks very high on the list of bizarre events in Olympic history.'

Conditions on marathon day, at the height of a sweltering Missouri summer, were brutal, not to mention dangerous. Most of the 25-mile course was a dusty track wending its way over seven steep hills. The temperature topped 90°F and there was only one water stop allowed.

That was bad enough. But the organisation of the race further reduced it to farce and near-disaster. The runners set off from the Olympic stadium in the wake of a large group of horsemen briefed to keep spectators away from the competitors. In the stifling heat, the runners began struggling to breathe amid clouds of dust kicked up by the animals' hooves.

Worse was to come. Race officials, pressmen, trainers and doctors were meant to follow the runners in their cars, but somehow managed to overtake them. Now the hapless athletes were running in 90°F heat, breathing in a noxious cocktail of exhaust fumes and dirt.

Despite such adversity, Lorz, a 24-year-old New Yorker and member of the Mohawk Athletic Club, sprinted to the front. But after just nine miles he was spent, collapsing almost unconscious at the roadside. His manager bundled him into his car and set off in the direction of the stadium and the finish line.

Meanwhile, various strange sub-plots were being played out. With Lorz in the back of a car, the pace was being set by a Cuban postman, Felix Carvajal – fit as a fiddle and presumably used to the tropical heat. The crowds' darling, Carvajal had already had an epic journey even to make it to the Games. To fulfil his dream of competing at the Olympics, he had run repeatedly around the central square in Havana until he attracted a crowd, then stood on a soapbox and begged for contributions, insisting that he would win gold for Cuba. He raised enough for his trip but, on disembarking in New Orleans, gambled away the lot. He was then forced to hitch lifts and beg for food before finally arriving in the Olympic city, where a New York cop taking part in the discus took a shine to him and looked after him.

Carvajal turned up to the marathon in long trousers, a long-sleeved shirt and smart shoes. His discus-throwing friend hacked off the trouser legs and sleeves with scissors, but Carvajal was stuck with the shoes, more suitable for a night out in Havana than a 25-mile race. Not that they seemed to impede him. He raced along cheerfully, bantering with spectators in his pidgin English and playfully stole two peaches from an official to quench his thirst. Occasionally, he ran backwards.

Carvajal was on course for the unlikeliest of victories until he spotted an apple orchard. Leaping the fence, he scoffed a succession of green apples before rejoining the race. The sour fruit checked his progress, causing severe stomach cramps and, at the 18-mile point, he left the course to find a toilet.

Meanwhile, Lorz had had a ten-mile lift to recover from his exhaustion. The car eventually overheated and broke down, but he now felt refreshed enough to rejoin the race. Running the last five miles to the stadium, he broke the finishing tape to thunderous applause, 'winning' in a time of 3 hours, 13 minutes.

Lorz posed for a picture with President Teddy Roosevelt's daughter Alice, who placed a laurel wreath around his neck. But just as he was about to receive his gold medal, the terrible truth about his 'race' spread like wildfire among the crowd. They hurled abuse at Lorz, who tried desperately to pass it all off as a practical joke.

At the very moment he was being unmasked as a fraudster, another athlete, Thomas Hicks from Massachusetts, staggered into the stadium, delirious, exhausted and covered in dust.

His own progress there was barely legitimate. He had been close to collapse ten miles from the finish, but his manager slipped him a bizarre mixture of strychnine sulphate, egg whites and brandy. Fuelled by chemicals and with alcohol masking his pain, Hicks limped along to the finish, occasionally stopping for a top-up each time he felt ready to quit.

Finally, somehow, he crossed the finish line – in 3 hours, 28 minutes and 53 seconds – and was declared the winner, Lorz by now having been disqualified. Hicks was in a sorry state; in fact, he was close to death. His friend Charles Lucas said of him, 'His eyes were dull, lustreless. The ashen colour of his face and skin had deepened. His arms appeared as weights well tied down. He could scarcely lift his legs, while his knees were almost stiff.'

Doctors worked for several hours to save his life, and the next day he was only too keen to announce his retirement, adding, 'I would rather have won this race than be President of the United States.'

A Frenchman came second; third came an American, Arthur Newton, said to be have been robbed of gold in Paris four years earlier by a French rival who knew short-cuts through the city. Carvajal, the plucky postman from Havana, came fourth, despite his tummy trouble.

Only 14 of the 31 starters finished. One runner, William Garcia of San Francisco, was found near death, the lining of his stomach apparently destroyed by inhaling dust.

Bizarrely, two of those who finished were not even meant to have taken part. They were African students Len Taunyane and Jan Mashiani, who were actually in St Louis to pose as Zulu tribesmen in a Boer War exhibit. Len finished ninth despite being chased off the course by a vicious dog and having to find his way back through a cornfield. Jan came twelfth.

As for cheating Lorz, he was banned from all competitions, only to be reinstated soon afterwards. Just a year later, in 1905, he won the Boston Marathon in a creditable time of 2 hours, 38 minutes and 25 seconds... and he ran all the way.

• The 1904 marathon was only the third in the Games' modern history, but incredibly, Lorz's cheating wasn't the first of its kind. In the first marathon, in 1896, Spiridon Belokas of Greece took bronze, riding part of the way in a carriage. He was rumbled, and disqualified.

BLOODY NERVE
Roberto Rojas

No attempt to cheat an opponent of victory was more fiendishly conceived, more brazenly executed or more disastrous than that of the Chilean goalkeeper Roberto Rojas. Rojas, with his team facing defeat and elimination from the 1990 World Cup, slashed his head open with a razor blade, pretending he had been brained by a firework thrown by a Brazilian fan. The idea was to get the game abandoned and force a replay or Brazil's disqualification. And it almost worked.

The crucial qualifying match on 3 September 1989 attracted an immense crowd of 160,000 to the Maracanã stadium in Rio de Janeiro, Brazil. At stake was a place at Italia '90 – and while Brazil could go through with a draw, Chile had to win.

Brazil were 1-0 up with 23 minutes left when an attractive 24-year-old Brazilian secretary named Rosemary de Mello joined in the carnival atmosphere in the stands by hurling a flare on to the pitch near the Chilean goal. 'I didn't mean it,' she said, after her arrest. 'I didn't even know what would happen when I pulled the string.'

For Rojas, it was a golden opportunity. With the flare still smouldering a yard from him, he collapsed to the ground, holding his head, from which blood was now pumping. The game was halted and, as the Chilean team carried their stricken goalie off the pitch, they insisted they could not play on in such perilous conditions.

The crowd stayed put for two hours, hoping the match would restart, but it was abandoned.

Outraged Chileans poured on to the streets of their capital Santiago and, with car horns blaring, laid siege to the Brazilian Embassy in protest at the assault on their national goalkeeper. Military police threw up roadblocks to quell the riot. Back in Rio, the Chilean team reported that 31-year-old Rojas needed five stitches for an inch-long cut to his eyebrow.

FIFA, football's international governing body, had a crisis on its hands. Its rules did not cover such an occurrence. Normally, if a team refuses to play or leaves the field before full time, it forfeits the match. Simple. But the regulations said nothing about what to do if a team fled for its life. The least FIFA could do, it seemed, was order the tie to be replayed at a neutral ground. Chile had already been allowed to do this when an earlier away match had been threatened by crowd trouble.

This seemed like the right solution to soccer's sages, among them Bobby Robson, then England's manager, who saw the game on TV. 'The only fair answer for the players would be to replay the game in a neutral country,' he declared. A second, admittedly extreme, alternative for FIFA was to disqualify Brazil from the tournament and send Chile to Italy.

Either would have been a triumph for Rojas. But doubts were already being expressed in Brazil about the severity of his wound and the manner in which it was sustained. Officials who saw him claimed he was not seriously hurt at all and that the Chileans were merely using it as an excuse.

Brazilian doctors questioned why, if he had been hit by a firework, he was not burned.

Rojas's Brazilian club, Sao Paulo, needed no further evidence. They immediately terminated his contract and stuck him on the transfer list. 'Rojas would certainly encounter hostility from Brazilian supporters and could tarnish the image of Sao Paulo,' a spokesman said.

'They want to turn me, the victim, into the accused,' bleated Rojas.

FIFA studied the referee's report, video footage and photographs of the incident and interviewed witnesses before concluding that the firework never struck Rojas. He had taken a dive, they said. FIFA awarded the match to Brazil, and upped the scoreline to 2-0 for good measure. Rojas was banned from the game for life and Chile – already now out of the 1990 World Cup – were barred from the 1994 tournament, too.

FIFA boss Sepp Blatter said the team was guilty of 'the biggest attempt at a swindle in the history of FIFA', branding Rojas's conduct 'criminal'. But even at that stage, he didn't know the full extent of the cheating. That took nine months to emerge, when Rojas, who had kept goal in the second half with a razor blade hidden in his glove, finally came clean to a newspaper, saying he could no longer live with the guilt.

'I cut myself,' he said. 'I cut myself just once, but it must have been deep because there was a lot of blood.'

Rojas served 12 years of his life ban before it was lifted in 2001. His redemption was complete when, in 2003, he was made coach of Sao Paulo, the Brazilian club which had thrown him out in disgrace. He said this of the repercussions after his night of shame in Rio: 'It was a serious mistake and everyone closed the doors to me. I was judged and I was harshly criticised. I had to prove that I wasn't a bad character because of one mistake.

'But the first step to restarting life is to recognise the mistake. First, I had to reconquer myself as a person. I couldn't spend my whole life being guilty.'

As for Rosemary, the firework thrower, the scandal provided her with an unexpected career opportunity. She was talent-spotted by *Playboy* and became a nude centrefold.

JUST NOT CRICKET
WG Grace

The 'spirit of cricket' is a byword for fair play. Anything untoward in any area of life is 'just not cricket'. But how was this reputation born, when the father of the modern game, WG Grace, was such a first-class bounder and cheat?

William Gilbert Grace was a colossus of the noble game. Over 43 years, from 1865 to 1908, he scored 54,896 first-class runs, including 126 centuries, and took 2,876 wickets. He captained England and played his last Test match at the ripe old age of 51. All this on tricky, uncovered, unprepared pitches that today's cricketers wouldn't be seen dead on.

A doctor by profession and powerfully built at 6ft 2in, WG was an imposing character who intimidated opponents and umpires. His personality was larger than the game itself – and he knew it. Ticket prices doubled if he played. Notices outside grounds read: 'Admission 3d. If Dr W G plays, 6d'.

WG was determined that spectators should get value for their money – and let's hope it was this altruism, rather than mere egotism, that led to his most famous and most blatant act of cheating during a charity match. Given out LBW first ball, WG refused to budge, telling the flabbergasted bowler: 'The crowd came to see me bat, not to see you bowl.'

In fact, the Gloucestershire giant often refused to leave the crease even when obviously and legitimately out. He was known for stooping to replace the bails if bowled, claiming they were simply blown off by a freak gust of wind, not dislodged by the impact of ball on stump. One fearless umpire stood his ground, gave WG out and said, 'Let us hope that the wind helps the good doctor on his journey back to the pavilion.'

Sometimes, the manner of his dismissal was so comprehensive that even WG could not argue. In 1898, the Essex fast bowler, Charles Kortright, clean-bowled the legendary batsman in spectacular style, removing two stumps. In an early example of the fine art of 'sledging', Kortright told Grace, 'Surely, you're not going, Doc? There's still one stump standing!'

The underhand tactics WG employed to preserve his wicket were rarely subtle. After playing the ball in the air, he would routinely distract the fielder trying to catch him by bellowing, 'Miss it!'

In the field, he was similarly unsporting, chattering away to distract a batsman as the bowler delivered the ball. One batsman had the audacity to hit each of the last four balls of a Grace over for six. When the umpire called 'Over', Grace is said to have told him to shut up and continued bowling – the unfortunate batsman getting out off the seventh delivery.

Grace's gamesmanship may have indirectly given birth to the tradition of The Ashes. After fielding a ball during the 1882 Oval Test against Australia, Grace paused long enough for the batsman, Sammy Jones, to assume the ball was 'dead' and meander up the pitch to tap down a divot with his bat. Grace hurled the ball at the stumps and ran him out. After the innings, the Aussie fast bowler Fred Spofforth burst into the England dressing room, called Grace a cheat, and stormed, 'This will lose you the match.'

Fired up, Spofforth took seven wickets for 44 runs, bowling England out eight short of their victory target of 85. The defeat was humiliating – England's first on home soil – and prompted a journalist to write his now-famous obituary for English cricket, saying its body would be cremated and the ashes taken to Australia.

Despite his own indiscretions, Grace had an acute sense of fair play when he was the victim of a perceived injustice. He once used his skills as a medic to stitch the wounded eye of an opposing wicket-keeper, only for the patient to stump him off the next ball. Grace turned on the hapless keeper and snarled, 'After all I've done for you, that's what you do to me.'

Perhaps WG's most outrageous act was the day he kidnapped an Australian Test cricketer, padded up and ready to bat at Lords, before dragging him across London to play instead for Gloucestershire.

Billy Midwinter was eligible to play for both sides since he had been born in Gloucestershire before emigrating Down Under. Unfortunately, he had committed himself to play for both on the same day, and unsurprisingly opted to turn out for his country against Middlesex at Lords rather than his county at the Oval five miles away.

Grace, skippering Gloucestershire, was incensed to find himself a man short. He left the Oval, caught a Hansom cab to Lords and burst into the Aussies' dressing room. There, he and two team-mates are said to have bribed Midwinter into joining them, and the four hurried back to the Oval. On arrival, they had a stand-up row with the Aussie captain and several team-mates, who had taken another cab to South London in hot pursuit.

Grace's argument was that Midwinter had committed himself first to the county and had been paid more by the Australians to turn out for them. He told them, 'You are a damned lot of sneaks.'

Even by WG's standards, kidnapping was sharp practice. But as the Aussies might have said, 'Cheats never prosper.' Midwinter made four and a duck as Gloucestershire lost. The Aussies flourished without him, winning handsomely.

GOALFLINGER
Roy Carroll

So widespread is cheating in football, and so low our expectations of players' moral standards, that when Manchester United's Roy Carroll blatantly scooped the ball out of his goal to avoid a 1-0 defeat to Spurs, the only questions asked were of the referee, the linesman and whether video replays should be introduced.

Heaps of abuse were poured on the hapless officials for failing to notice that the ball had indeed been a yard over Carroll's line, as every spectator in that area of the ground and viewers on television could see all too easily. The ball had been hoofed from the half-way line and although the linesman ran after it as fast as he could, he was still not best placed to judge exactly what had happened.

The controversy occurred during injury time in a Premiership match at Old Trafford on 4 January 2005. With the sides deadlocked at 0-0 and a minute or so to play, Spurs midfielder Pedro Mendes speculatively punted the ball 50 yards in the direction of Carroll, who was stranded off his goal line. Carroll ran back in time, but fumbled the ball over his shoulder and into the goal. It bounced a good three feet behind the goal line, whereupon Carroll dived back and scooped it out on to the field of play.

The incident was considered a howler by Carroll and little more. Debate raged instead over the shortcomings of Premiership referee Mark Clattenburg and more particularly his assistant Robert Lewis.

Niall Quinn, commenting for Sky Sports, called Lewis's blunder the worst he had seen during his 22 years in football. Alan Hansen was similarly furious on the BBC. Lewis was forced to defend himself by saying, 'By the time the ball landed, I was still 25 yards away and it was impossible to judge if it had crossed the line. There was nothing I could have done differently, apart from run faster than Linford Christie.'

What no one – bar a tiny band of newspaper columnists – ever said was that Carroll could simply have admitted the ball had gone in and the goal would have stood. He would have cost his side the game but he would have remained honest.

But then no one seriously expected a footballer to be honest. Not with Premiership points, places in Europe, vast salaries and reputations at stake. Carroll's cheating was entirely acceptable as far as football was concerned – it was up to the officials, and perhaps the use of technology, to uncover the truth. As the *Daily Telegraph* pointed out: 'The poor chap was no more programmed to charge upfield imploring the ref to award an own goal against him than a dog is to walk straight past a lamppost.'

Simon Barnes, chief sports writer of *The Times*, was prepared to call a spade a spade, however, beginning a comment piece with this simple verdict: 'Roy Carroll is a cheat.'

MARATHON BY RAIL
The Berlin 33

Athletes are often banned for taking drugs. But 33 got banned for taking a train during a marathon. It is unknown whether they planned their scam all along, or whether it was cooked up as they wearily trudged the first half of the race in Berlin in 2000. But at some point around the 15-mile stage, the sneaky gang left the course, dodged down into the city's underground network and caught a train, emerging at another station somewhere near the finishing line. Then they duly finished as though nothing untoward had gone on.

But there was no hiding place from technology – they forgot that each runner was carrying a microchip recording their time every 3.1 miles. After the race, organisers checked the microchip records – and 33 of those who finished the 26.2-

mile course were found to have no times to speak of for the last 11 miles. All were disqualified.

Kenyan Simon Biwott stormed to victory in 2 hours, 7 minutes and 42 seconds, unaware he was racing train passengers.

THE HAND OF GOD
Diego Maradona

Diego Maradona – ever after known as 'Dirty Diego' – dumped England out of the 1986 World Cup with as overt an act of cheating as has ever been seen on a football field. The resulting outrage was eclipsed both by his surreal explanation and the sublime second goal he scored four minutes later.

Tensions were already high between England and Argentina before the quarter-final which would make football history. The Argentines were still holding a grudge over the controversial sending-off of their captain Antonio Rattin in the 1966 quarter-final against England... as well, of course, as their defeat in the 1982 war over the Falklands.

Some 114,580 spectators at Mexico City's Aztec Stadium watched an absorbing but goalless first half. Then, five minutes into the second, England defender Steve Hodge sliced a looping pass back to

Peter Shilton that forced the goalkeeper to run out and punch clear.

Hoping to beat Shilton to it, Maradona, Argentina's 25-year-old star striker, ran forward and leapt in the air. At a little over 5ft 5in he was unlikely to head the ball beyond the outstretched fist of 6ft 1in Shilton, so he extended his own left arm and punched it over him into the open goal.

England's players protested furiously and were ready to take the free-kick they were sure would be awarded for handball. To their horror and incredulity, Tunisian referee Ali Bennaceur was pointing to the centre spot – it was 1-0. Neither he nor his linesman saw anything improper.

At the press conference afterwards, Maradona coined one of football's most famous phrases. The suspect goal was scored, he said, '*un poco con la cabeza de Maradona y otro poco con la mano de Dios*' (a little with the head of Maradona and a little with the hand of God).

It was another 14 years before he held his hand up, so to speak. 'Now I feel I am able to say what I couldn't then,' he said in his autobiography. 'At the time, I called it "the hand of God". Bollocks was it the hand of God... it was the hand of Diego! And it felt a little bit like pickpocketing the English.'

Maradona also revealed he used Argentina's

wounded pride over the Falklands to justify his cheating to his sceptical team-mates. Even they were dubious about the goal and hesitated before embracing him. 'I told them, come hug me or the referee isn't going to allow it. They were quite timid. They came over to embrace me but it was as if they were saying, "We've robbed them,"' he said. 'But I said to them, "Whoever robs a thief gets a 100-year pardon." It was something that just came out of me. It was a bit of mischief.'

Mischief it might have been to Maradona, but England were in uproar. Manager Bobby Robson spat, 'You don't expect such decisions at World Cup level.'

But even he could not hide his admiration for what Maradona pulled off next.

Four minutes after handling the ball into the net, he won it again ten yards inside his own half. The little wizard spun 180° past two England players, sprinted down the touchline past a defender, then another, dodged Shilton and a last despairing tackle from a defender before sliding the ball into the open net. It has since been voted the greatest goal in the history of the World Cup – and dubbed the 'Goal of the Century' – and it sealed England's fate, despite the consolation they scored later.

In ten seconds, Maradona had run more than 60 yards and beaten six England players to score. In one now famous sentence, the veteran TV commentator Barry Davies summed up the mood as England fans' loathing for Maradona's dishonesty was transformed into a grudging respect for his genius. 'Oh! You have to say that's magnificent,' he said.

In defeat, manager Robson echoed the mood. 'Today, Maradona scored one of the most beautiful goals you'll ever see. That first goal was dubious; the second one was a miracle, a fantastic goal. It's marvellous that every now and then the world produces a player like Maradona.'

Ironically, Maradona – who went on to win the World Cup – credited the honesty of the English team with enabling him to score such a wonder-goal.

'I don't think I could have done it against any other team because they all used to knock you down,' he said. 'The English are probably the noblest team in the world.'

Two decades on, the goal sparked a bitter public row between ref and linesman, with the latter claiming the former should never have allowed it. 'He was an idiot, more fit to herd camels in the desert than take charge of a World Cup game,' said Bulgarian Bogdan Dotchev. Dotchev, of course, failed to wave his flag to rule the goal out at the time, but he insisted it was not his place to do so. 'With the ref having said the goal was valid, I couldn't have waved my flag and told him the goal wasn't good – the rules were different back then,' he said.

Nonsense, according to Keith Hackett, head of referees in the Premiership, a man who took charge of nearly 100 internationals in the 1980s and 1990s. 'There were no rules at the time which said this linesman could not alert the referee to a handball,' he said. 'This incident was one of incompetence on the part of the officials.'

THE FAST AND THE FURIOUS
Michael Schumacher

Based on statistics alone, Michael Schumacher is the greatest Formula One driver who ever lived. The German won more world drivers' championships and more Grand Prix than anyone else. No one ever drove more fastest laps or achieved more pole positions. He was utterly ruthless, yet cool-headed.

Three hugely controversial incidents hang over his great career. Two involve collisions – the first of which robbed Britain's Damon Hill of the world title. On a third occasion his car came to a halt on the circuit preventing his closest rival from taking pole position the following day.

The incident with Hill at the 1994 Australian Grand Prix in Adelaide caused worldwide shock. The men were bitter rivals. Schumacher had said he 'did not respect Hill as a driver or a man' and claimed the Briton was only a challenger because his more gifted team-mate Ayrton Senna had been killed in a crash that season. Hill retorted, 'Michael's not my favourite person. I'm going to beat the pants off him. I know I can win the title.'

Adelaide was the last race of the season and would decide the world championship. Schumacher was a single point ahead of Hill, and leading the race, when he suddenly veered off the track and hit a wall. Although he steered back on and kept the lead, he was going slowly enough for Hill to overtake him on his inside. At this point the German's car drove into Hill's path. Both cars were damaged and forced to retire, and since neither driver scored a point, Schumacher won the title.

Hill somehow remained dignified. 'I knew Michael had everything to gain should neither of us finish the race,' he said. 'I don't think he did anything that I wouldn't have expected. I think he would have made it difficult for me to pass in any situation. That's understandable. After all, we were racing for the world championship.'

But the fury directed at Schumacher in Britain

was intense. The *Daily Mirror* ran a campaign demanding justice for Hill and amassed thousands of messages supporting him and condemning Schumacher. The German's defence was that he had trouble steering after hitting the wall. 'We just ran over each other. That's racing,' he said. Of the British public's reaction, he said, 'They are allowed their opinion.'

Race stewards studied the crash and concluded it was a normal racing accident. They took no action.

There was a similar incident in 1997, this time against the Canadian driver Jacques Villeneuve at the European Grand Prix at Jerez, Spain, in front of a global TV audience of 350 million.

Yet again, it was the last race of the season. Again, Schumacher had a one-point lead in the drivers' championship. Again, he was leading the race. But this time the result didn't go his way. As Villeneuve tried to overtake him on the 48th lap, their cars collided – but the Canadian soldiered on, finishing third and winning the title, while Schumacher had to retire from the race.

The media were in uproar. 'Jacques Villeneuve is world champion because Michael Schumacher tried to cheat his way to Formula One's richest prize,' roared Stan Piecha, veteran motor racing correspondent of the *Sun*. Schmacher added, 'His reputation is tarnished beyond repair.'

There was similar anger in other British papers, of course. But this time even the Germans joined the fray. The daily paper *Bild* said, 'He played for high stakes and lost everything – the World Championship and his reputation for fair play.' A paper in Frankfurt branded him 'a kamikaze without honour'.

The Italians were mortified that Schumacher was representing their team, Ferrari. The daily paper *Unita* said of him, 'The driver covered himself, Ferrari and Italian sport as a whole with shame.' It demanded he be replaced with a new driver with 'a real sense of morality'.

Schumacher robustly denied these claims. He argued he had simply made an error in the heat of the moment. 'I am human like everyone else and unfortunately I made a mistake,' he said. 'I don't make many but I did this time.'

His punishment from motor racing chiefs was a meaningless slap on the wrist – his points for the season were scrubbed. They concluded he was guilty of a 'serious error' but that his 'manoeuvre was an instinctive reaction and, although deliberate, not made with malice or premeditation'.

In May 2006, Schumacher had driven the fastest lap in the build-up to the Monaco Grand Prix and was heading for yet another pole position. But the reigning world champion Fernando Alonso was roaring up behind him and about to beat his time. Schumacher's Ferrari stalled at the penultimate corner and the car was left on the track. Race officials waved yellow warning flags, forcing Alonso to slow down and thus ruining his lap time.

Yet again, Schumacher insisted it was a simple mistake. 'I did not cheat,' he said. 'Anyone who thinks that was not a mistake should try driving round Monaco. I pushed too far and it stalled.'

A fierce debate ensued. Keke Rosberg, world champion in 1982, said, 'Does he think we are all fools or idiots? No way was it an error. He parked the car in the middle of the road. It disgusts me.'

Villeneuve, survivor of the 1997 crash with Schumacher, said, 'He should not be allowed to race a car if he does this type of thing.'

Renault boss Flavio Briatore, Alonso's manager, said, 'He did not hit the barriers, he just parked the car. What he did was unsporting, astonishing, incredible.'

Britain's three-times world champion Sir Jackie Stewart chipped in as well. He said. 'When you see it in slow motion, he had plenty of time to do something.'

This time, the protests bore fruit. Stewards scrapped the German's time and made him start the following day's race at the back of the grid – although he still managed to finish fifth. The stewards' statement concluded, 'We can find no justifiable reason for the driver to have braked with such undue, excessive and unusual pressure at this part of the circuit,' it said. 'We conclude he deliberately stopped his car in the last few minutes of qualifying when he had thus far set the fastest time. This is a breach of the 2006 Formula One Sporting Regulations Article 116.'

Schumacher retired from Formula One after the 2006 season at the age of 37 and having reportedly become a billionaire. He always maintained his innocence and said he was consistently the victim of smears by rival camps. 'Your enemies believe one thing and the people that support you believe another thing,' he said.

RACE FROM THE FINISH
Rosie Ruiz

When Rosie Ruiz won the 26.2-mile Boston marathon in 1980, she apparently had one crucial advantage over her exhausted rivals – she had neglected to run 25.7 miles of it. Ruiz, officials said, joined the race by vaulting the crowd barrier with just half a mile to go and sprinted to the finish.

She recorded the third-fastest marathon time in history by a female (2 hours, 31 minutes and 56 seconds). But still, incredibly, it took race officials the best part of a week to change their minds and strip her of the winner's medal.

Ruiz, it must be said, denies to this day that she cheated, insisting she ran the entire course and won fair and square. No one has come forward to say they remember seeing her during the race, other than those who witnessed her joining it at the end. Not one race monitor saw her at any of the checkpoints. Not one of the hundreds of photos taken on the day features Ruiz. Since she denies cheating, the controversy may never be settled.

Ruiz qualified to run in Boston at the New York marathon six monhs earlier. A female photographer named Susan Morrow says she saw Ruiz on a subway train during that race, with a sprained ankle. The pair took the train together to the finish line, where Ruiz was led away for medical treatment. It is believed that first-aiders wrongly marked her down as a finisher (and why not, she was at the finishing line), thus qualifying her for Boston.

Officials believe that on the day of the Boston race, she either walked or got the subway to within a half-mile of the finish. Suspicions were raised by her inability to recall any landmarks on the course as well as her total ignorance of common marathon jargon.

Ruiz, eventually stripped of her title, refuses to

this day to hand back her medal. Now living in Florida, she claims she has been offered substantial sums to tell her story in a book but has refused them.

A few years after the race, she came face to face with the official winner, Canadian Jackie Gareau, who set a course record in Boston only to find Ruiz already on the podium. Ruiz approached Gareau at a race in Miami, still defiantly claiming her victory. 'I recognised her,' said Gareau. 'I said, "Why did you do that?" I thought she was acknowledging that she made a mistake, but she said no, she ran it and she would do it again.'

DIVE OF THE CENTURY
Rivaldo

Diving in football is so prevalent it could merit a book of its own. But if one example stands above all others for its shamelessness, it is the play-acting by Brazilian star Rivaldo that sickened the world in 2002.

This was no mere exaggeration, no 'Hollywood' dive to incriminate a mistimed tackle. This was brazen dishonesty before a worldwide TV audience of millions. Rivaldo, hit in the shin by a ball kicked at him by a petulant Turk, paused momentarily, then suddenly clutched his face as if shot, before falling to the ground. The weak referee sent the Turk off.

One might have expected better of Rivaldo, one of history's greatest players and a former World Player of the Year. But South American football apparently has different values from those elsewhere – though the rest of the world is catching up fast. Conning the referee has no stigma there – it is entirely meritorious if the result goes your way. Brazil's football vocabulary includes terms like '*malandragem*' (cunning and naughtiness) and '*esperteza*' (cunning and craftiness) – both legitimate ploys.

Rivaldo's cheating was by no means the first in the World Cup match between Brazil and Turkey in South Korea on 3 June 2002. Another con trick, and further poor refereeing, handed Brazil the penalty that would decide the game. Turkey had taken a surprise lead on 47 minutes, only for the Brazilians to draw level three minutes later. It remained 1-1 until three minutes from time when a Brazilian player, Luizao, was fouled outside the penalty area. Luizao delayed his inevitable collapse until he was inside the penalty area and, when he heard the ref's whistle, placed the ball on the penalty spot as though a penalty was a foregone conclusion. The duped ref sent off the

Turk and duly awarded the penalty, which Rivaldo scored to put Brazil 2-1 up.

As Luizao said later, 'I had to use a little *malandragem*. He was pulling on me, and I waited 'til we got to the area to go down. As soon as I heard the whistle, I picked up the ball and put it on the spot.'

Three minutes later came the incident for which the game is particularly remembered. With Turkish hopes of an equaliser fading by the second, Brazil were awarded a corner. Rivaldo, blatantly time wasting, dawdled by the corner flag so long that a Turkish defender, Hakan Unsal, could take no more and hoofed the ball in anger at him.

Jaws dropped around the world as Rivaldo's blatant deception was replayed on TV, including inside the Munsu Stadium which resounded to jeers and booing. Football fans had seen play-acting before, of course, but nothing like this. FIFA had promised to crack down on cheating before the tournament and fined him £5,000 for 'simulation'. But the 30-year-old player was entirely unrepentant. 'This is something that will never end in football,' he announced. 'I'm calm about the punishment, and I am not sorry about anything. These things happen in football... I was both the victim and the person who got fined. Obviously, the ball didn't hit me in the face, but I was still the victim. Nobody remembers what that Turk did to me. He deserved to be sent off. Of course, he didn't get me in a place where I could be hurt, but you don't do the sort of thing he did. I was glad to see the red card come out. It doesn't matter where the ball hit me – it was the intent that mattered.'

Rivaldo concluded with this gem: 'The World Cup will be better if there were more referees like that. Great players must be able to protect themselves if football is to stay the Beautiful Game. There is too much foul play and violence in football today.'

The Turks were incensed. Their national football president Haluk Ulusoy condemned Rivaldo and the Korean referee Kim Young-Joo. 'Rivaldo fell down like he was having a brain haemorrhage, despite the ball hitting his leg,' he said. 'It was acting, and FIFA told us any action designed to fool a referee would be punished. But it's our players who are being punished.' Referring to the Korean War of the 1950s, he added, 'We sacrificed a thousand soldiers here to defend Korea, and one Korean has now killed 70 million Turks. I wish I were not forced to speak about a Korean in that way. We love them as people, but that man can't be a referee. In Turkey, he would not even be allowed to take charge of a second division match.'

The Brazilian full-back Roberto Carlos spelled

Just not cricket: WG Grace, father of the modern game and first-class
bounder and cheat.   © *Popperfoto*

Above: Liverpool's Bruce Grobbelaar concedes one of three goals against Newcastle in 1993 for which the *Sun* claimed he took £40,000.

Below: The camera never lies. Manchester United's Roy Carroll kept mum about conceding a clear goal against Tottenham Hotspur.

Dis-onischenko: Boris Onischenko lived by the sword and saw his Olympic dream die by the sword as he was caught in a cunning act of cheating in the fencing competition.

© AP

Above: England captain Douglas Jardine sets an aggressive leg-side field for his controversial Bodyline tactic in the 1932-33 Ashes series.

© *Getty*

Below: Ray Illingworth and Mike Atherton face a daunting interrogation from the press following the 'dirt in the pocket' affair.

© *Times Newspapers Ltd*

The not-so beautiful game…

Above: Rivaldo shamelessly clutches his face as if being shot – he was actually struck in the shin by the ball – in order to get his Turkish opponent sent off during the 2002 World Cup.

© *BBC*

Below: The infamous 'hand of God' goal.

© *Empics*

Danny Almonte, the Little League baseball superstar outed as a 14-year-old. The maximum age for a Little League player is 12.   © *AP*

Above: Smarter than the average team … many of the 2002 Spanish Paralympics basketball players had perfectly normal IQs.   *© AP*

Below: Greg Chappell, arm aloft. But he certainly wasn't above underhand – or rather underarm – tactics in the 1981 series against New Zealand.

© News Group Newspapers

Above: Talented cyclist Michel Pollentier's 'ingenious' ruse to beat the drug testers saw him busted and banned from the sport.

© *AFP/Getty Images*

Below: Bitter rivals Michael Schumacher and Damon Hill collide, ending Hill's title hopes and drawing widespread condemnation in Britain of the German driver.   © *Offside/L'Equipe*

out why gamesmanship was a crucial part of his team's tactics. 'Imagine, if we are losing 1-0 in the 90th minute and somebody nudges me in the penalty area, of course I'm going to fall over and get a penalty to level the game,' he said. 'It could well be the most important match of my life.' Referring to the four stars on the Brazil shirt, each representing a world title, he said, 'In football, you have to use a bit of cunning. Brazilian footballers are cunning. This is why we have four stars on our chests.'

Chapter 2

Nobblers

THE FELLING OF THE ALL BLACKS
Suzie the Poisoner

Rugby's 1995 World Cup Final was like a movie script – the host nation, South Africa, beating the mighty New Zealand All Blacks in extra time before an ecstatic sell-out crowd, then receiving the trophy from the country's first black President Nelson Mandela in one of the iconic images of the entire history of sport.

Except it was all rather murkier than that.

Just before the match in Johannesburg on 24 June, more than half the Kiwi squad was struck down by food poisoning. It was obvious they were suffering physically – their performance on the field was well below their normal standard – and they lost 15-12.

They were, and remain to this day, convinced they were nobbled. They even named a mysterious waitress, 'Suzie', as the saboteur who slipped an unknown substance into their water at the team hotel.

The All Blacks' then coach Laurie Mains hired a private eye to investigate. The detective reported back that a betting syndicate in the Far East paid Suzie to spike the water.

The South African guard assigned to the team backed the claims up. Rory Steyn, a former head of security for Mr Mandela, said the All Blacks had 'definitely been poisoned'. Mains replied, 'I'm relieved that someone of such importance in South Africa has acknowledged that the food poisoning occurred. It's comforting for the entire All Black party that was there.'

At the time, the Johannesburg hotel's management said the source of the illness might have been bottles of chilli sauce the players had in their rooms.

But eight years later, they put forward a more shocking theory, which served only to fan the flames. They claimed the Kiwi stars poisoned *themselves* on the night before Saturday's game by eating dodgy prawns at an illicit dinner in a local restaurant behind the coach's back. When they got sick, they were too frightened to admit how and where it happened and instead blamed shifty Suzie. As hotel boss Tony Rubin said, 'There was no Suzie... I never met Suzie. She didn't exist. We knew what had happened with the players after going to the restaurant, but the hotel took a decision not to talk about the incident.'

Mains, the Kiwi coach, was outraged. 'That is a total fabrication. The team were sick on Thursday night, not Friday. I can absolutely assure you that on Friday night, the players were still receiving treatment. It's just another attempt at a cover-up.'

Mains said the seafood meal Rubin referred to happened after the Final, on the Sunday night, and involved all the players and the management. 'We all went out and had a real seafood pig-out,' said Mains. 'Mr Rubin needs a better memory.'

Suzie or no Suzie, there were other incidents that made the Kiwis' hotel stay less than conducive to a stellar performance in the final – including a seemingly orchestrated cacophony of car alarms ringing out as they tried to sleep.

Years later, the Kiwi skipper, Sean Fitzpatrick, claimed the South Africans were desperate for a final against the All Blacks... and were similarly desperate to win it.

ICE SCREAM
Tonya Harding and Nancy Kerrigan

It was, as one American magazine editor said, 'the biggest story since the assassination of President Kennedy'. And while that may have been the excitement of the moment, the nobbling of top ice skater Nancy Kerrigan by the associates of her rival Tonya Harding did shock the world. The story had the makings of a classic thriller. Oddly enough, it also had the makings of an opera.

Kerrigan and Harding were top-class US ice-skaters and polar opposites – Kerrigan, the pretty, well-spoken, all-American girl from Boston on the east coast; Harding, the stumpy, cigarette-smoking, trailer-park chav, raised in grinding poverty in the north-west.

In early 1994, their fortunes were heading in different directions. Harding's best year had been 1991, when she won the US title and came second in the World Championships. Since then, her form had gone south. Over the same period, Kerrigan's had improved – she was the reigning US champion and looking likely to hold on to the title.

When they arrived in Detroit for the US championships in January, both women had their eyes on the ultimate prize – the gold medal at the Winter Olympics in Lillehammer, Norway – then only a month away. It wasn't just for the glory. There was a fortune to be made. An Olympic champion could expect to pick up £300,000 a show once back in the US. The stakes were high and the rivalry intense. Harding said of Kerrigan, 'I'm going to whip her butt.'

Kerrigan, 24, was already pulling in big money from endorsements, and performed in designer dresses. By contrast, Harding, 23, was hard up and forced to sew her own threadbare outfits. Kerrigan seemed to have it all. She was among the favourites for the US and Olympic titles; Harding was thought too erratic to stand a chance in either.

The plot to cripple Kerrigan was hardly a masterpiece of subtlety. On Thursday 6 January, she was being interviewed after a training session at the Detroit rink by journalist Dan Scarton when a tall, masked man in a leather jacket rushed up. Before the stunned skater could utter a sound, the man crouched down, whacked the back of her right leg with a metal pipe and fled. 'Nancy just started screaming and sobbing,' said Scarton. 'She said, "It hurts. It hurts so bad. I'm scared."'

Kerrigan sat down on the ice, repeatedly howling 'Why me?' The answer, the world initially assumed, was that she was the target of another crazed fan, as the stabbed tennis star Monica Seles had been a year earlier.

Kerrigan's leg was swollen and badly bruised, enough to rule her out of the US championships, which, in her absence, Harding went on to win.

But within days, detectives made a shocking announcement: They suspected the attack was arranged by Harding's ex-husband, with whom she was reconciled, and her bodyguard. Harding denied any involvement, insisting she was disappointed that Kerrigan had pulled out of the championships. 'I really wanted to skate against her,' she said.

Harding's ex, Jeff Gillooly, denied everything. 'I wouldn't do that. I have more faith in my wife than to bump off her competition.' Her bodyguard, a 25-stone dimwit named Shawn Eckhardt, said, 'I would never get involved in anything like that.'

The conspiracy's solidarity was quickly crumbling, however. The truth was that Gillooly and Eckhardt had hired an Arizona-based hit-man, Shane Stant, to carry out the nobbling. Another man, Derrick Smith, was employed as his getaway driver. When he was not paid on time, Stant became angry and the truth started to leak out. A church minister in Portland, Oregon, was mysteriously given a tape of Gillooly and Eckhardt plotting to maim Kerrigan with Stant's help.

The FBI arrested Gillooly, who immediately implicated his ex-wife Harding, claiming she was in on the nobbling from the outset – something she denies to this day. Harding did admit knowledge of the plot – but only after the attack. She also confessed that she had kept quiet, something she deeply regretted. However, with unbelievable gall, she said she saw no reason for that to rule her out of taking her rightful place as US champion in the Olympic team for Lillehammer. 'Despite my mistakes and my rough edges, I have done nothing to violate the standards of sportsmanship expected in an Olympic athlete,' she said.

Harding even threatened to sue for millions if she was kept out of the team – and she duly went to the Games. So, too, though, did Kerrigan, who, by mid-February, had healed sufficiently to compete again. To deafening cheers, she came a triumphant second, while Harding, skating like a baby elephant, came a tearful eighth.

Back home, Harding pleaded guilty to obstructing the police investigation and was fined £63,000. She was ordered to serve 500 hours of community service, serving up meals-on-wheels, tidying graveyards and trimming grass verges, and put on probation for three years. She was banned for life from skating and stripped of her US title. In a masterpiece of understatement, a disciplinary panel said Harding's actions 'undermined the concept of sportsmanship and fair play'.

Bodyguard Eckardt – described by the judge as 'infamous, notorious, greedy, dishonest, even stupid' – was jailed for 18 months. Stant and Smith got the same. Gillooly was locked up for two years and fined £70,000. He was driven by 'ruthless ambition and raw greed', the court heard. His voice trembling, Gillooly said, 'I would say to anyone considering entering into a desperate act, as I did, to think again. Because I did not, I am going to prison. I have apologised to Nancy Kerrigan and I am sorry. For my actions, I take responsibility.'

He also bitterly reasserted that Harding was involved from the start. 'I'm the fall guy,' he said. 'Anybody half-way intelligent knows she was involved.'

Harding repeated her denial. 'There was never any rivalry between Nancy and me,' she said. 'We were friends and, sometimes, when we were away with the US team and had to share rooms, I would pick Nancy. We roomed together maybe ten times. I knew her mom and dad, too. They were really nice.' She said she discovered the truth 'a day, maybe two' before the FBI swooped on Gillooly. 'Jeff and his gang were talking and I was eavesdropping from the bedroom,' she said. Asked why she failed to report them to police, she said, 'I had been threatened. If I had done that, I wouldn't be sitting here today. Eventually, I went to my attorney, and when the police agreed to give me protection, I told them.'

With skating now out of bounds, Harding, voted America's most hated sports personality in one poll, was left to trade on her notoriety. She landed a movie role, raced cars and eventually became a boxer – as well as an unwilling porn star, thanks to the leaking of a video Gillooly made when they were first married.

Kerrigan, now a mother, runs several charities and is a skating commentator. More than a decade on from the scandal, she said this: 'It was a very dark period. Why would somebody do something like that? It's hard to explain. Someone got obsessed with wanting to do better and be ranked higher. I just happened to be a part of it, a victim in it.'

In 2006, *Nancy and Tonya: the Opera*, written by award-winning author Elizabeth Searle, made its debut in Boston. Searle said, 'It's amazing that, 12 years on, there is still great fascination. Not just in the United States, but around the world. Harding and Kerrigan come across as primal types, the princess and the bad girl. America is full of Tonyas who want to be Nancys. It is perfect for opera.'

43

THE £10 MILLION TUMMY BUG
Tottenham Hotspur Football Team

When ten Tottenham Hotspur players were stricken with a stomach bug before losing a crucial game worth £10 million, the fear was that they had been nobbled. But forensics experts cleared the suspect lasagne they ate at the team hotel – the illness was a simple virus. How, then, did shady gambling syndicates in the Far East manage to make a fortune on the surprise result of the match?

Tottenham needed to win the away game at West Ham on the last day of the 2005/06 season to ensure a higher Premiership finish than bitter rivals Arsenal. It would have clinched for them a lucrative place in the Champions League for 2006/07.

The night before the match, the north London club checked into the upmarket Marriott Hotel at Canary Wharf and ate dinner. In the early hours, several players began vomiting.

Manager Martin Jol was woken at 5am with the bad news. At 7am, Tottenham chairman Daniel Levy was told up to ten players were stricken by suspected food poisoning. Spurs tried to get the game postponed, but the Premier League said they still had enough fit players to go ahead.

Some of the sick stars played anyway but were

visibly off their game. Midfielder Michael Carrick was 'barely able to stand', according to one report. Spurs duly lost 2-1 while Arsenal beat Wigan to scoop the Champions League place.

Conspiracy theories were rife. Had the players been poisoned as part of a betting sting? They were certainly expected to beat West Ham – and there was big money to be made if they lost.

Spurs considered suing both the Premier League and the hotel. The difference between a Champions League spot and a UEFA Cup place was worth some £10 million. It was a serious business, and police forensic experts were called in to take samples of the lasagne.

But samples of a different sort taken from the sick players showed they had Norovirus, a viral gastroenteritis, the symptoms of which take as long as 48 hours to emerge. The players had got sick just a few hours after eating dinner – so the meal could not have been to blame.

Dr Alex Mellanby, an expert in communicable diseases, said, 'The affected cases would have been exposed to the virus before they visited the hotel and the infection was probably transmitted from person to person.'

So that was that – a simple virus.

But something was still suspicious about it all, as a *Sunday Times* investigation revealed a week later.

The players had started to vomit in the early hours. Their absence from breakfast was noticed by hotel staff at 8am, around the same time as heavy bets were placed in the Far East on West Ham to win. The mass illness was not made public until 12.15pm.

A lawyer working for a London bookmaker told the newspaper, 'The big money on West Ham started just before 8am. Serious chunks of cash were being waged, enough to win £1 million or more on a single bet. Millions will have been won in Asia.'

So what gave the gamblers the confidence to bet so heavily on the underdog four hours before the Spurs stomach bug was announced? Inside knowledge? We will doubtless never know.

Chapter 3

Fixers

GUIDED BY SATAN
Hansie Cronje

Hansie Cronje's fall from grace was the most spectacular and perhaps the most tragic in the history of sport. The squeaky-clean, devoutly Christian South African cricket captain – a revered all-round player and a national hero – was banned from the game for life after dragging it into the worst corruption scandal in its history. It is a mark of what he achieved before his disgrace that, after his death in a plane crash aged 32, he was still voted the 11th-greatest South African of all time, higher even than anti-apartheid activist Steve Biko.

Cronje's downfall was greed, as he eventually

admitted once he finally owned up to the match-fixing and bribery in which he was involved, and into which, more damagingly, he lured two of his players.

He had been such a towering, upstanding figure as a captain and an ambassador for post-apartheid South Africa that the allegations against him were at first treated with derision. He appeared, from his public image, the last cricketer on Earth likely to be guilty of such a thing.

An Afrikaner from Bloemfontein, Cronje was a born leader, groomed as the future South African captain from his first international appearance in 1992. He got the job at 25 – a grim-faced and ruthless skipper on the field, but a prankster off it. The respect he earned from his men bordered on hero-worship.

Under him, the national team played 53 Test matches, winning 27, drawing 15 and losing 11. Cronje had great talent with the bat, scoring six Test centuries and averaging 36.41 over 68 matches. He was an impressive and sometimes explosive one-day player, too, and he was no slouch with the ball, taking 43 Test wickets at a respectable average of 29.95 runs each. There were few more formidable figures in the world of cricket.

But the edifice came crashing down in April

2000 when police in Delhi, India, suddenly announced they had a tape of Cronje passing on confidential information via mobile phone to a contact from a shady Indian betting syndicate.

The conversation was said to have taken place the previous month, as South Africa played India in a one-day series. Cronje and his contact agreed that opening batsman Herschelle Gibbs should score less than 20 in one particular innings. Cronje also said that, at some point in the series, he would open the bowling with his off-spinner Derek Crookes, a highly unusual move for any skipper and one that Crookes later admitted left him astonished.

In the face of such career-threatening accusations, Cronje began lying immediately. 'I am stunned,' he said. 'The allegations are completely without substance. I have been privileged to play for South Africa since 1992 and I want to assure every South African that I have made 100 per cent effort to win every match that I have played.

'I have never received any sum of money for any match that I have been involved in and have never approached any of the players and asked them if they wanted to fix a game.'

The head of South African cricket, Dr Ali Bacher, had no doubt about his innocence, especially since unsubstantiated rumours of match-fixing had emerged from India before. Dr Bacher said, 'I have spoken to Hansie and he says it is absolute rubbish. He is known for his unquestionable integrity and honesty.'

Four days later, Dr Bacher was woken at 3am by a phone call. It was Cronje, highly emotional and ringing to confess that he had not been 'entirely honest' in his original denials. He admitted taking up to $15,000 from a London bookie, not for match-fixing, but for 'forecasting' results. Even this was a long way from the truth, but it was enough to get Cronje sacked as captain and for Bacher to eat humble pie. 'We are shattered,' he said in a statement. 'The United Cricket Board and the Government have been deceived.'

Gradually, a trickle of damaging evidence began. Doubts were expressed over an unprecedented decision Cronje had taken to forfeit an innings in a Test against England to set up a crowd-pleasing run chase and produce a result in a match heading for a draw. England won it. And once Cronje's disgrace became public, South African batsman Daryll Cullinan said, 'I would like to think Hansie was acting in the best interests of the game and doing something for the public, but it totally went against the guy I knew. He wasn't in the habit of giving something to the other side or making a game of it.'

Next came the story of how, back in 1996, Cronje, apparently half-joking, suggested throwing a one-off match against India in exchange for $250,000 – a proposal which the team rejected.

Indian police then produced more evidence – that Cronje took an £85,000 bribe to fix one-day matches in India.

Then came an extraordinary statement from Cronje. A devout Christian since 1994, when he accidentally killed a young black girl in his car, he blamed all his dodgy dealings on Satan. 'In a moment of stupidity and weakness, I allowed Satan and the world to dictate terms to me,' he said. 'I have been a role model for many people in South Africa and this was a lesson for all of you. When Satan comes knocking on the door, always keep your eyes on the Lord Jesus Christ. The moment I took my eyes off Jesus, my whole world turned dark and it felt like someone had stuck a knife through my chest.

'Thank you, Mum and Dad – I apologise for letting you down. I'll be back, better off than I am now, once I have been punished.'

A commission of inquiry, led by Judge Edwin King, was set up to get to the truth of the scandal. It was there that Gibbs, once Cronje's prolific opening batsman, did his disgraced skipper the most damage. Visibly distressed, Gibbs described how, before a one-day match against India at Nagpur, Cronje came into the hotel room he was sharing with the fast bowler Henry Williams 'with a big grin on his face'. 'He said, "Someone can pay you $15,000 if you score less than 20,"' Gibbs recalled. 'Henry was just getting out of the shower and Hansie told him he could get the same amount for bowling his ten overs for not less than 50. Henry said yes.' Cronje also told the pair that South Africa needed to make less than 270 in total.

Gibbs accepted the captain's offer, telling the inquiry that all along he was thinking of his mother, whom he would need to support following her divorce from his father.

Like Cronje, Gibbs had lied about the bribes when the evidence first emerged. 'I was scared and uncertain, and I was protecting Hansie,' he said, adding that Cronje had repeatedly ordered him to keep lying.

Gibbs did not get his money – because he 'forgot' about the deal. Instead of making less than 20, he smashed his first two balls for four and scored 74 from only 53 deliveries. When Cronje came out to bat, he asked the captain, 'What do we do now?' Cronje said that in order for the total to be less than 270, he would throw away his wicket – but in the end they made 320. Williams, the fast bowler, failed to achieve his bribe 'target', too, sustaining a shoulder injury that prevented him from bowling more than 11 balls.

Cronje finally faced the inquiry and came clean, to a point. He said the 'Satan' he referred to earlier was his own 'unfortunate love of money', which he said was an addiction. He said he was 'driven by greed and stupidity and the lure of easy money'. His evidence also implicated two other international captains, Salim Malik of Pakistan and India's Mohammad Azharuddin, both of whom are covered later in this book.

Cronje said he was first approached by a shady character named only as John before a one-day game against Pakistan in Cape Town on 10 January 1995. He offered Cronje £6,500 to lose the game but Cronje turned him down. Cronje said he believed John was the same crooked Indian bookie who paid Australian stars Shane Warne and Mark Waugh thousands of pounds for pitch and weather information a few months earlier (a misdemeanour which Aussie cricket chiefs covered up for four years, despite fining both players).

Cronje said when he and Malik went on to the field to toss the coin before play, the Pakistan captain asked if he had spoken to John, and plainly knew him.

Cronje said he turned down another approach at the start of South Africa's tour to India in 1996 but was finally lured into a web of corruption by Azharuddin. 'On the evening of the third day of the third test at Kanpur, I received a call from Mohammad Azharuddin,' Cronje said. 'He called me to a room in the hotel and introduced me to Mukesh Gupta – 'MK'. Azharuddin then departed and left us in the room. MK asked if we would give wickets away on the last day of that Test to ensure that we lost. He asked me to speak to the other players and gave me approximately $30,000 in cash to do so.'

Cronje claimed he did not approach any of his players to ensure defeat, but South Africa lost anyway and he 'effectively received money for doing nothing'.

Later, he refused an offer of £100,000 to throw a one-day international, but when India toured South Africa the following year, he took money for supplying information on team selections. During one Test, he got £30,000 for telling MK in advance the total at which he would declare South Africa's innings closed. Cronje also mentioned a London bookie called Sanjay who handed him a box stuffed with American dollars in exchange for match information.

During the fateful tour of India in 2000, Sanjay repeatedly pestered Cronje to fix matches. 'Calls would come through to my room as late as three o'clock in the morning,' Cronje said. 'It became increasingly difficult to resist his requests to manipulate results.'

Eventually, he said, he agreed to try to fix the game in Nagpur for £80,000.

Cronje said he earned £5,000 and a leather jacket from a bookie calling himself Marlon Aronstam after his surprise forfeiture of an innings against England. 'He told me he was a cricket lover and wanted to see some action on the field. He urged me to speak to Nasser Hussain, the English captain, about an early declaration to make a contest of it, saying this would be good both for me and for cricket.

'Marlon said if we declared and made a game of it, he would give £50,000 to a charity of my choice and would also give me a gift.'

Cronje denied throwing the game and insisted he genuinely thought South Africa had every chance of bowling England out in the resulting run chase. He said, 'Marlon visited me in my hotel the following evening and gave me a leather jacket and £5,000.' Cronje made clear that Hussain, England's skipper, knew nothing of the deal.

Reading out a statement to the inquiry, Cronje said, 'Words cannot begin to describe the shame, humiliation and pain which I feel in the knowledge that I have inflicted this on others. To my wife, family, and team-mates in particular, I apologise.'

It was not enough for some of the players he betrayed, including fast bowler Allan Donald – so often encouraged by Cronje to bowl his heart out for their country. 'It's incredible,' said Donald. 'It's just greed, really, that's made him do this.'

The fact that he sucked Gibbs and Williams into his plot was probably most damaging to Cronje. They were both non-white players, and Cronje was a champion of the cricket development programme that nurtured young black talent.

Cronje was led from the inquiry in tears. 'I hope I can put the money to good use to try to redress the wrongs I have done to my game and my country,' he said. 'There is no excuse and I have let the team, the fans and the game down.'

The disgraced cricketer was further humiliated after requesting an audience with former President Nelson Mandela, who gave him a piece of his mind. Mandela said later, 'It is my duty to say to him, "You have made a serious mistake."'

Cronje was banned for life from any involvement with cricket, including media work. Gibbs and Williams were banned from international cricket for about six months.

In his first interview about the scandal, printed in the *News of the World*, Cronje admitted suicide had crossed his mind. 'I open my eyes and wonder how I am going to get through the day,' he said. 'Yes, there were dark moments when I wondered if it was still worth living. I'd think, "Hansie, you have fallen so far anyway. A few more feet won't matter." It's not a pleasant experience going from being a national sporting icon to the most reviled man in sport, especially when the only person to blame is myself.'

His marriage to Bertha survived, despite him lying to her about where the money was coming from. And, as months went by, Cronje began successfully rebuilding his life. The all-encompassing ban on him was softened to allow him to work as a cricket journalist. He even began to harbour a wild fantasy that he might one day return to coach the national side. 'I think that, one day when it comes along, I would certainly like to have that, because I certainly tried my entire career to make South Africa the number-one cricket-playing country in the world,' he said. But it was obvious the authorities would never allow it and he sought out a new career, becoming a finance manager for a building firm, while also studying for a masters degree.

On Saturday 1 June 2002, Cronje missed a scheduled flight home from Bloemfontein to the city of George and hitched a ride on a cargo plane.

Approaching George, the two pilots lost visibility in a storm and crashed into mountains. They and Cronje died instantly.

The country's cricket bosses paid a magnanimous tribute, despite his betrayal of them. President Percy Sonn said, 'Hansie was an excellent cricketer and a very popular and successful captain, who led his team to some great achievements. He gave much to cricket in this country.'

Cronje's priest, Pastor Ray McCauley, said, 'He was a person with a huge heart and, whenever I rang him, he would go with me to orphanages and schools. Once the match-fixing broke and he was not allowed to play cricket again, he took it on the chin and never complained about it.'

South Africans were divided between those who could forgive him and those who could not. A survey of thousands of people for a TV series on Great South Africans placed the disgraced cricketer 11th, ahead of some hugely important figures in the nation's history.

More than 2,000 mourners attended his televised funeral at the Bloemfontein school where he was once captain of cricket and rugby. Hundreds of tearful pupils chanted 'Hansie, you are still our hero... ' as his coffin passed. Former South African cricketer Peter Pollock told the congregation, 'What Hansie did was wrong. But

God forgives the repentant sinner. He stood with no excuses. He took his medicine.'

Peter's son Shaun, who assumed the captaincy stripped from Cronje, paid an emotional tribute to an inspirational leader and friend. Choking back tears, he said, 'H, we'll miss you.'

INDIA'S MR FIXIT
Mohammad Azharuddin

Tall, elegant and suave, Mohammad Azharuddin was possessed of a batting talent that placed him among the élite of the game's history. He hit centuries in each of his first three Tests in the 1980s and rose to captain India throughout most of the 1990s. But even that still couldn't explain the extravagance of his lifestyle – the two £10,000 watches, the two luxury apartments, the expensive cars and clothes, the Bollywood actress wife. His estimated fortune was in the tens of millions of dollars. Indians often wondered where it came from... surely not just from cricket?

Hansie Cronje provided the answer. Coming clean after his own match-fixing shame was exposed, he ended Azharuddin's career at a stroke, naming him as the man who led him down the slippery slope to ignominy. The South African captain said that, in 1996, his Indian opposite number introduced him to the crooked bookmaker Mukesh Gupta, known as 'MK', who began to bribe Cronje to throw matches.

Alongside Pakistan's Salim Malik, MK was the central figure in cricket's match-fixing scandal. A former bank clerk with a gift for numbers, he became interested in the game in 1984 when live matches were televised in India for the first time. Walking home from work one day, he saw people placing bets by the roadside – and saw there was money to be made. He began as a small-time bookie and, within a few years, had made a fortune. In 1988, he made his first introduction to an international cricketer, the Indian batsman Ajay Sharma, the first in a long line that would lead to Azharuddin.

Cronje's brief indictment of Azharuddin was a godsend to India's Central Bureau of Investigation, already probing claims of match-fixing. They hauled in several bookies, who, under interrogation, further incriminated the star. Azharuddin had riled some of them by playing them off against each other and they were happy to settle the score.

Azharuddin was questioned by the CBI, too, and, despite his earlier furious denial of Cronje's claims, confessed to fixing two one-day matches at MK's behest, against South Africa in 1996 and Sri

Lanka in 1997. The CBI, though, didn't believe that was the full extent of it. 'This "admission" that he "did" only two matches for MK appears a dilution of the actual facts in the context of the amount of money he had received from MK,' one of the investigators said later.

Azharuddin also admitted throwing a one-day match against Pakistan in 1999, for another illegal Indian bookie. For that, he was paid £17,000. Again, the CBI was convinced there were many more dodgy games. 'In view of the large amount of money Azhar had received from an illegal bookie and the hospitality he has enjoyed through him, it is very difficult to believe that he did only one match.

'Cellphone printouts disclose frequent calls between Azharuddin and bookies, especially during matches. Azharuddin has accepted that he was provided a cell phone by bookies who also paid for his shopping at Harrods, London, in 1999 during the World Cup.'

As with Cronje, the most damaging revelations for Azharuddin were that he roped other players in on the plot. The CBI said, 'It is clear that Azharuddin contributed substantially to the expanding player/bookie nexus in Indian cricket. The inquiry has disclosed that he received large sums of money from the betting syndicates to fix matches, which resulted in this malaise making further inroads in Indian cricket.'

Azharuddin, then 37, was barred from cricket for life. But in 2006, to general dismay elsewhere, India's cricket chiefs said they were contemplating lifting the ban. 'The general opinion is that Azhar has undergone enough punishment,' a spokesman said.

As for MK, a man seemingly unknown to cricket pundits before 2000, despite his long and malign influence on the game, he disappeared back into the shadows.

CAPTAIN CROOK
Salim Malik

The seeds of cricket's match-fixing scandal that erupted in the late 1990s and led, in 2000, to the downfall of three international captains, were sewn by Salim Malik.

He was a Pakistani middle-order batsman of consummate grace and skill. In 1982, at just 18, he made a century on his Test debut and another 14 of them over the 103 Tests he played.

But it was after his elevation to Pakistan captain in the early 1990s that he became involved with the Indian bookmakers who were to blight the sport. One Test in particular blackened his name for good, against Australia at Karachi in September 1994. Pakistan won the match, but five months later Australians Shane Warne, Mark Waugh and Tim May claimed Malik tried to bribe them to throw the game. Malik denied it and a war of words with the Australians dragged on for four years.

Pakistan cricket chiefs investigated the claims first. Then a full judicial inquiry was launched. Warne, the best spin bowler in history, finally gave evidence in 1999 and told of this encounter with Malik before the final day of the Karachi Test. He claimed, 'Salim said he needed to talk to me. I was surprised and asked him what he wanted to speak to me about. He said it was private and confidential and asked me to come up to his room. He insisted that I come up to his room.

'Salim was staying in the same hotel. I went up to his room. He was by himself. He said, "How are you, Shane? Are you enjoying the tour? I've got something very important to talk to you about."

'I said, "Oh yeah, what's that?"

'He said, "Look, we can't lose tomorrow."

'I said, "What do you mean, you can't lose tomorrow?"

'He said, "I don't think you understand. Our pride is at stake. Everything is at stake. We can't lose this first Test."

'I said, "Well, mate, our pride is at stake, too. I'm

sorry to tell you this but we're going to whip you blokes tomorrow."

'He said, "I don't think you understand what I am asking of you. What I want is for you and Tim May to bowl wide of the off stump and bowl poorly, so that the match is a draw, and for that I will give you and Tim May $200,000. I can have it in your room in half-an-hour."

'I said, "What the hell is going on here? What do you mean? What are you talking about? I don't understand." I thought he must be joking. I said to him, "You've got to be kidding." I asked him if he was serious.

'He said, "I am serious. You must get back to me." I told him to get lost in the strongest possible fashion.'

Mark Waugh, one of Australia's classiest batsmen of recent decades, said Malik made another approach at a function in Rawalpindi a month later, allegedly offering money to fix a one-day international the next day. Waugh said, 'He came up to me and offered $200,000 for four or five players in the Australian team to play badly and lose the game. I was shocked. The next day I told Mark Taylor because, as captain, he would inform the relevant people.'

Australia won the game.

The two-year judicial inquiry heard a mass of

evidence against Malik from players and officials. Most damning was that of his former vice-captain Rashid Latif, who claimed Malik summoned him to his hotel room before a one-day international against New Zealand at Christchurch in 1994 and offered him £12,500 to throw the match. Latif made similar allegations relating to a 1994/95 tour of South Africa and Zimbabwe. He quit the team in protest when nothing was done.

The inquiry took months to rule on Malik's fate. It was still pondering when the Hansie Cronje scandal broke – and when a *News of the World* investigation exposed Malik still further. Undercover reporters posing as high-rolling punters hoping to make a killing on cricket trapped him into promising to rig an upcoming Pakistan–England Test series for £500,000 a game. Malik allegedly told the journalists he could entice players to throw the match, and knew bookies who would pay a fortune for knowing the fix was in. 'I'll introduce you to an Indian bookie – it all happens in India – he'll come here to meet you,' he said.

Malik spoke about other fixed matches he knew of, but claimed white players could not be trusted in any illegal enterprise. Shane Warne, for instance, 'grassed us up', he said.

Days later, the inquiry announced its findings

and recommended Malik, then 33, be fined £12,500 and banned for life from any involvement in cricket, which he duly was. The report concluded, 'Everyone seems to name him as the main culprit in match-fixing – his own coaches, managers and fellow players.'

MOCKERY OF A MATCH
West Germany v Austria

WEST Germany and neighbours Austria produced the most shameful football match in history – lamely going through the motions to end a World Cup tie with the 1-0 scoreline both teams needed, as 40,000 spectators bayed for their blood.

The result seemed contrived deliberately to eliminate underdogs Algeria from their first ever World Cup. This went down badly with the crowd's many Algerians, who had to be restrained from invading the pitch and taking both teams apart.

Algeria had pulled off one of the great upsets in football history by beating the mighty West Germans 2-1 in the opening match of Group 2 in the 1982 tournament in Spain. The Germans, Austria and Algeria all beat Chile, while the Austrians beat Algeria. So with only one game left – West Germany v Austria – Austria and Algeria were level on four points, with West Germany on two and Chile none. This meant the Germans had to beat Austria to qualify for the next round. Having already beaten Chile heavily, their goal difference was bound to be better than Austria's or Algeria's. Austria would qualify in second place even if they lost, so long as they kept the margin of defeat below three goals. In other words, a West German victory by one or two goals suited them both.

The match that followed in La Molinon stadium, Gijon, on 25 June 1982, was a scandalous, degrading sham, a 'disgusting charade' in the words of the *Sun*, which demanded both nations be expelled from the competition.

It began normally enough, with the Germans piling on the pressure to secure their win. They duly scored in the tenth minute, and that's where the game effectively ended.

With an agreeable 1-0 scoreline in place, players simply stopped competing. For 80 minutes they strolled along, passing the ball aimlessly. Neither side attempted a shot or header. If anyone felt rash enough to make a challenge, they shook hands afterwards and pulled their opponent to his feet. With 25 minutes to go, bored Austrian players were seen asking their bench how long the game had left. In the 66th minute, the Germans brought on a midfielder to replace their star striker Karl

Heinz Rummenigge, presumably in case the European Footballer of the Year suddenly could bear no more and scored. The game duly finished West Germany 1, Austria 0 and Algeria went out.

The spectators were howling abuse, whistling and waving white handkerchiefs. They chanted '*fuera, fuera*,' – Spanish for 'get out'. Police with guns and dogs moved in to quell a riot and a threatened pitch invasion from the Algerian contingent in the stands.

The *Sun*'s veteran sports writer John Sadler, who watched the game, said, 'If ever a football match looked pre-arranged, this was it. If ever football's credibility took a savage and sickening kick in the stomach, it happened in Gijon before 40,000 witnesses.'

Algerian soccer chief Ben Ali Sekker said, 'We will file an official protest with FIFA and demand disqualification of West Germany and Austria because they violated the principles of sportsmanship by their lack of ambition.'

There was no evidence that the match result was pre-arranged and FIFA could do nothing. However, the scandal did bring about a change to World Cup rules. From then on, the final round of games in each group was played simultaneously so teams could never fix a result to suit them both.

BALLPARK FIGURES
The 'Black Sox' Scandal

The fixing of the World Series in 1919, arguably the most famous scandal in the history of sport, involved a conspiracy by Chicago White Sox players to throw baseball's biggest prize in exchange for bribes from mobsters. The series of nine games lasted only eight as Chicago, favourites to beat the Cincinnati Reds, lost by five games to three. It was the equivalent of a top football team plotting to lose a Premiership title decider on the last day of the season. The US scandal sent shockwaves around the world and has inspired or influenced dozens of books and movies in the nine decades since.

The catalyst was low pay. It is hard to imagine now, but in those days even the biggest stars of a very lucrative sport were on wages far below their market value and had no union to improve their lot.

The problem dated back 40 years. In 1879, just three years after America's National League was founded, a newly established 'reserve clause' allowed clubs to hang on to their players even after their annual contracts expired. The idea was to ensure clubs could keep their five best players, but it was soon expanded to take in the entire squad and was cynically used by clubs to prevent stars switching to other teams for a pay hike.

By 1919, the White Sox – run by a notoriously mean owner, Charles Comiskey – were one of America's élite teams. The players disliked Comiskey, and morale over pay was low. Indeed, a story did the rounds at the time that Comiskey's penny-pinching was so extreme he made the players launder their own uniforms – and that the Black Sox nickname they eventually earned through corruption in fact pre-dated the scandal, referring instead to the grubby state of their white uniforms.

The team was further divided by class – the poorly educated and working class were paid less than their more schooled team-mates, and the two factions barely spoke. The combination of all these factors was incendiary.

The year 1919 was one of renewal and optimism in America. Optimism, mainly, that things couldn't get worse. The First World War had claimed almost 120,000 American lives. That toll was dwarfed by the 500,000 killed by the 1918 'Spanish 'Flu' pandemic, which claimed 30 million victims worldwide.

The war in Europe had impacted on baseball, too – with several star players drafted and attendances down. So, in 1919, the sport benefited from a huge renewal of interest as Americans looked to a bright future beyond sickness and war. Match attendances more than doubled, from 3 million in 1918 to 6.5 million the next year. Records were broken on the field, too – Babe Ruth of the Boston Red Sox hitting 29 home runs, the most in a single season.

At the season's end, the winners of the American League, Chicago, and the National League's winners, the Cincinnati Reds, met for the World Series. The format, normally a best-of-seven games, was increased to the best of nine, reflecting the upsurge in the sport's popularity.

The key figure in the conspiracy was White Sox First Baseman Arnold 'Chick' Gandil. The fix was his idea – and he contacted a friend, professional gambler Joseph Sullivan, to investigate its feasibility.

Enter the New York-based Jewish mob boss Arnold Rothstein, a legendary criminal figure who has since inspired several fictional characters – Meyer Wolfsheim in *The Great Gatsby* and Nathan Detroit in *Guys and Dolls* – and is admired by characters in the movie *The Godfather II*.

One of the fathers of American organised crime, Rothstein was a skilled gambler who, although he would later profit enormously from bootlegging and drugs during Prohibition, was already a millionaire by 1919. It was he who would bankroll the fix, even though he managed later to convince a Grand Jury that he 'turned down flat' the idea.

Sullivan, having secured Rothstein's funding through his contacts, gave Gandil the go-ahead and promised that every player he roped in would share £100,000. To put that sum in perspective, Gandil's annual salary was $4,000, although less talented players than him were earning twice that in lesser teams.

Gandil recruited five team-mates – pitchers Eddie Cicotte and Claude 'Lefty' Williams, outfielders 'Shoeless' Joe Jackson and Oscar 'Happy' Felsch, and infielder Charles 'Swede' Risberg. Another infielder, Fred McMullin, heard about the scam and demanded a cut in exchange for keeping quiet. One player, Buck Weaver, was approached but refused to take part. His failure to report the conspiracy was to prove his undoing.

Cicotte was a crucial player with an extra motivation. He had a clause in his White Sox contract guaranteeing him a whopping bonus of $10,000 for winning 30 games in the season – but he was rested after 29 wins in a ruse he suspected owner Comiskey of concocting to avoid paying him. Cicotte needed the money badly – he had a wife and children to support on top of a large mortgage for a farm he had bought in Michigan. He eventually agreed to Gandil's plan, provided he was paid $10,000 up front.

The plotters met in a New York hotel room that Gandil rented. Years later, Gandil described that fateful summit: 'They all were interested and thought we should reconnoitre to see if the dough would really be put on the line. Weaver suggested we get paid in advance – then if things got too hot, we could double-cross the gambler, keep the cash and take the big end of the series by beating the Reds. We agreed this was a hell of a brainy plan.'

Word spread among the gambling community that the series was fixed, and bets poured in on underdogs Cincinnati. The rumours reached the press, with sports reporters vowing to watch individual performances like hawks for any signs of foul play.

Cicotte received his $10,000 bung before the first game on 1 October in Cincinnati. For safe keeping, he sewed it into the lining of his jacket. Although some of his co-conspirators played well that day to avoid arousing suspicion, Cicotte duly had a stinker and cost Chicago the game. Rothstein had told Cicotte to hit the first Cincinnati batter with a pitch as a sign the fix was going ahead. Cicotte's second pitch did just that.

By that night, the conspirators' solidarity was already crumbling. Only Cicotte had been paid.

Two intermediaries acting on the players' behalf demanded their cut from an aide to Rothstein but he produced none. Meanwhile, owner Comiskey was growing suspicious and took his concerns to the heads of both the American and National leagues. Since his team had lost the first game, they dismissed him as a bad loser.

The plotters carried on with the fix in the second game, with errors by Gandil and pitcher Williams in particular costing Chicago dear. Now 2-0 down, the conspirators had still seen little of their promised money and the plot was in disarray. Chicago then won the third game.

Gandil insisted the players got some money or they would try to win Game Four, too. He was given $20,000 and they lost the game, thanks once again to deliberate errors by Cicotte. At one stage, he even jumped to intercept a ball from Jackson which would have resulted in an 'out' for Chicago. Gandil later admitted ordering Cicotte to do it.

The plotters divided up their loot. The 3-1 scoreline became 4-1 when Cincinnati won again in Game Five, this time due mainly to blunders by Felsch in the field.

When another $20,000 they were promised failed to materialise, the Chicago players decided enough was enough. They won both Games Six and Seven, making the score 4-3. It was far too close for comfort for Rothstein and his associates, who were furious. The mob boss personally had at least $270,000 on Cincinnati to take the series.

The night before Game Eight, Williams, due to pitch for Chicago, was bluntly warned by a shadowy mob figure that unless he threw the game he and his wife would be killed. Williams' performance the next day was duly abysmal, and Cincinnati took the game and the World Series.

Not all the conspirators had underperformed. Jackson had a World Series record 12 hits, a superb batting average and the only home run of the series. But this would not eventually be enough to save his career.

Rumours of the fix were rife at the club and throughout baseball during 1920, fuelled by newspaper speculation. Despite his own suspicions, Comiskey publicly denied any fix. 'I believe my boys fought the battle of the recent World Series on the level, as they have always done,' he said. 'And I would be the first to want information to the contrary if there be any. I would give $20,000 to anyone unearthing information to that effect.' In private, he hired an investigator to probe the finances of the suspected conspirators.

Almost a year after the World Series, the rumours

and suspicion had finally become irresistible and a Grand Jury was convened. Cicotte tearfully came clean, telling the jury, 'I don't know why I did it. I must have been crazy. I needed the money. I had the wife and the kids. The wife and the kids don't know about this. I don't know what they'll think. I've lived a thousand years in the last twelve months. I would have not done that thing for a million dollars. Now I've lost everything – job, reputation, everything. My friends all bet on the Sox. I knew, but I couldn't tell them.'

Joe Jackson was next to talk, implicating Gandil and Williams during a two-hour statement. A famous story, which the star player always denied, tells how, as he walked from the courthouse, a wide-eyed youngster said to him, 'It ain't so, Joe, is it?' To which he replied, 'Yes, kid, I'm afraid it is.'

Comiskey suspended eight players in telegrams sent to each one. Williams then confessed to the Grand Jury. Felsch did the same in a newspaper. 'Well, the beans are spilled and I think I'm through with baseball,' he said. 'I got $5,000. I could have got just about that much by being on the level if the Sox had won the Series. And now I'm out of baseball, the only profession I know anything about, and a lot of gamblers have gotten rich. The joke seems to be on us.'

Rothstein's lawyer, William Fallon, decided the

mobster should face down the Grand Jury in Chicago in a bold plan to crush the rumours of his involvement. Rothstein said he was 'sick and tired' of being linked with the fix and said he had come 'to vindicate myself'. The tactic worked – incredibly, the investigators believed him.

The players were charged with various counts of fraud, and some of the most expensive lawyers in the State were hired to defend them. The trial began in June 1921 and the prosecution demanded a $2,000 fine and five years' jail for each man.

Despite a wealth of damning evidence, the players were found not guilty within two hours of the jury retiring to consider its verdict. This may have been because of the judge's bizarre insistence that they had to be proved guilty of conspiring 'to defraud the public and others, and not merely to throw ballgames' – a fine distinction if ever there was one. And there was more than a hint of suspicion that the jurors were starstruck. As the verdicts were read out, cheers erupted in court, hats flew in the air and some jurors lifted the players on to their shoulders.

The White Sox stars may have escaped jail, but their careers were finished. A new Commissioner of Baseball, Judge Kenesaw Mountain Landis – appointed to maintain the sport's moral integrity –

banned them for life with this statement: 'Regardless of the verdict of juries, no player who throws a ballgame, no player that undertakes or promises to throw a ballgame, no player that sits in conference with a bunch of crooked players and gamblers where the ways and means of throwing a game are discussed and does not promptly tell his club about it, will ever play professional baseball.'

The wide-ranging nature of the statement was enough to damn Buck Weaver, whose flawless performances throughout the World Series were used as evidence that he was not involved in the fix. He knew about it and kept quiet – for the judge that was bad enough.

All eight of the White Sox plotters were banished from Major League baseball. Gandil, the ringleader, became a plumber in California. In 1956, he gave his version of events in a magazine interview, claiming the players abandoned the plot early on because they knew they would be caught – and did their best to win. But the persistent rumours of the fix unsettled them and they played poorly anyway, he said.

As for Jackson, an all-time baseball legend and easily the biggest name caught up in the conspiracy, he maintained his innocence to his dying day. His many stellar performances during the 1919 World Series give that claim some weight. But there is no question he took money – even though his supporters counter that his lack of education and illiteracy made him unaware of the seriousness of the scandal he was mixed up in.

Shoeless Joe died in 1951, aged 63. His last words are said to have been, 'I'm about to face the greatest umpire of all. He knows I am innocent.'

BLACK WEDNESDAY
Peter Swan, Tony Kay, David Layne

When Bobby Moore was held aloft by his red-shirted team for a historic photo after the 1966 World Cup victory, one man was missing who should have been there. He was Peter Swan, one of three big stars of the Sixties jailed and banned from the game for what remains English football's biggest match-fixing scandal.

Swan, Tony Kay and David Layne played for Sheffield Wednesday, then one of England's élite clubs. Swan, the captain, had 19 England caps and was rated by some journalists as the world's best centre-half. Kay, a midfielder, was also an England international, albeit with one cap.

Layne was one of England's best young forwards.

In December 1962, 23-year-old Layne went to watch his old club, Mansfield Town, play West Ham and bumped into another ex-Mansfield player, a Scot called Jimmy Gauld. Gauld was secretly fixing matches, paying players to lose games and cashing in by placing bets on the result. He told Layne several players were making money by betting on the games themselves through him and that he was looking for another match to target. Layne said that Sheffield Wednesday seemed to be consistently losing to Ipswich Town, managed then by Alf Ramsay – later to lead England to World Cup glory. It seemed likely they would lose again in the upcoming away fixture at Ipswich.

The idea of a fast buck appealed to Layne, who, during training, roped in Kay and Swan. Each placed £50 with Gauld on Ipswich to win, which they duly did, and the players took home £100 in addition to their £50 stake.

Now comes the grey area. To this day, none of the three admits they threw the match. Sure, they lost the game, but they all insist the extent of their wrongdoing was placing the bet. Kay, for one, wasn't holding back on the pitch – he was rated Man of the Match in one newspaper the next day.

'Ipswich were one of those sides Wednesday

always struggled against,' Swan said later. 'I knew we were in for a hard time – I just thought we'd lose. It was the only bet we made. I said, "Let's get it on. We never do anything at Ipswich."'

Swan conceded that he was unsure whether he'd have thrown the match had his team been drawing or winning. 'We lost the game fair and square,' he said. 'But my money was on Sheffield Wednesday to lose and it would have been easy for me as a centre-half to give a penalty away or, if the ball was coming towards me, to turn it into the net.'

By the early part of the 1963/64 season, the *Sunday People* newspaper had exposed a match-fixing scandal in the lower leagues that involved as many as 200 players. As the net closed on Gauld, he decided to sell his story to the same paper and, in April 1964, exposed Layne, Kay and Swan using a taped conversation with the former.

All four men, plus seven other players from the lower leagues, were charged and tried in January 1965. Gauld got four years. To their bewilderment, the Sheffield Wednesday players were jailed, too – four months each – after being found guilty of conspiracy to defraud by fixing matches. The other players got between six and fifteen months.

The judge, Mr Justice Lawton, said of Tony Kay

— who, before the scandal broke, had become Britain's most expensive footballer in a £60,000 transfer to Everton – 'For £100, he has finished what is probably one of the greatest careers in football. He was tempted once, and fell.'

Prison was bad enough. But the most painful punishment came from the FA – a life ban for each. The trio couldn't even watch matches at any ground under FA jurisdiction. 'They chopped my legs off,' said Swan. 'Football was the only thing I could do.'

Kay never played again and lived in Spain for 12 years before returning home and becoming a groundsman. Swan and Layne made comebacks when the FA showed them mercy and lifted the life ban in 1973. Both were reinstated by Sheffield Wednesday – but, by now, they were in their 30s and the pace was too tough. Layne never got into the first team and Swan moved down to the Fourth Division. After retiring from the game, both ran pubs.

THE GREAT BUNGS BATTLE
Bruce Grobbelaar

To British football fans, Bruce 'Spaghetti Legs' Grobbelaar – named after his infamous 'wobbly legs' routine during the penalty shoot-out against AS Roma in the 1984 European Cup Final – was a household name as the Liverpool goalkeeper. He was sometimes erratic, often flamboyant and normally top-class. That all changed on 9 November 1994, when the *Sun* newspaper accused him of taking bribes to throw matches by letting in goals. The sensational allegation triggered an eight-year legal battle, at the end of which Law Lords upheld the decision that Grobbelaar had been defamed, but slashed the award of damages.

A Zimbabwean, Grobbelaar was, and remains, beloved among Liverpool fans. He effectively won them the European Cup in 1984 with his clowning antics during that penalty shoot-out against Roma. Two Roma players were so distracted as he knocked his knees together and went limp that they missed their spot-kicks.

At 37, with his career on the wane, Grobbelaar moved to Southampton and had been there only a few months when the *Sun* story broke. Under the headline 'WORLD EXCLUSIVE: GROBBELAAR TOOK BRIBES TO FIX GAMES', the paper claimed the star had taken £40,000 from an Asian betting syndicate to throw a game between Liverpool and Newcastle in November 1993. Newcastle had won 3-0 and the syndicate made more than £3 million predicting the score.

The paper further claimed that Grobbelaar was offered £175,000 to let in goals in other matches, but the results went against him and he could not cash in. The *Sun* caught him on video discussing fixing matches and accepting a £2,000 retainer from his former business partner Chris Vincent, who was posing as a middleman for a rival betting syndicate but was, in fact, exposing the star on the paper's behalf.

Grobbelaar issued an immediate denial. 'I have never tried to throw a game in my life,' he said, adding that the accusations would 'destroy me, my career, my marriage and my existence here'.

Police investigated and, four months later, arrested Grobbelaar, along with Aston Villa striker John Fashanu and Wimbledon goalkeeper Hans Segers, who were also said to have been involved. The three were tried in 1997 alongside a Malaysian businessman, Heng Suan Lim. In one famous piece of evidence, Grobbelaar was said to have admitted to Vincent that he missed out on a £125,000 'bung' for throwing a game against Manchester United because he made a 'blinding' save and the match was drawn.

But Grobbelaar claimed he was stringing Vincent along, and accepted his £2,000 only because he suspected his former partner was up to no good and wanted to expose him to the police.

The jury could not agree a verdict and, later that year, the four men faced a retrial, at the end of which they were dramatically acquitted. Grobbelaar, seemingly now in the clear, went on to win £85,000 libel damages against the *Sun* in 1999 but, two years later, three Appeal Court judges overturned the payout, saying it was 'an affront to justice'.

Lord Justice Brown branded Grobbelaar's various excuses 'absurd' and 'simply incredible'. Lord Justice Mathew Thorpe said he was corrupt 'to the hilt'.

But there was one more final twist in the story. Grobbelaar appealed to the Law Lords, Britain's highest court, who restored the original libel verdict. But they slashed his award from £85,000 to just £1, the lowest possible sum. The Lords said that the *Sun*'s specific claims, that Grobbelaar threw and attempted to throw games, were not proven. However, the senior Law Lord, Lord Bingham of Cornhill, said, 'He had acted in a way in which no decent or honest footballer would act, and in a way which could, if not exposed and stamped on, undermine the integrity of a game which earns the loyalty and support of millions.'

Lord Millett added that it was wrong if a man who took bribes to throw matches got damages 'merely because he cannot be shown to have carried out his part of the bargain'.

So Grobbelaar won £1... but he was ordered to pay the *Sun*'s legal costs of more than £500,000, which he could not do. Bankrupt and disgraced, Grobbelaar still hoped there might be some redemption. In 2005, he said, 'I believe I still have much to offer football. Maybe, one day, I will be able to coach my national team again.'

DIM SUMS
The Premiership Floodlight Scam

A betting syndicate's dastardly plot to force the abandonment of a Premiership match was exposed – but only after it had already made a fortune blacking-out two others.

The scheme was cooked up in Hong Kong, Malaysia and Singapore, where criminal gangs wagered tens of millions of pounds on Premiership matches they were able to watch through Sky TV.

The plan was simple. In Britain, a match is void if it is abandoned before the end. But under the betting rules in the Far East, the score when the match is called off is valid if it is already into the second half.

The syndicate generally targeted matches where one team was obviously stronger. The weaker side would be allowed a two-goal advantage. So if it was trailing by a single goal or drawing, it was 'winning' once the handicap was taken into account. The syndicate would bet heavily on the underdog and, if the result was in its favour at any point in the second half, it would pull the plug.

The logistics were trickier. The plotters needed access to the control room of each ground before the match to install a radio receiver capable of cutting power to the floodlights. This would be activated by a remote control held anywhere inside the ground. The device needed to be sophisticated enough so that ground staff could not merely find the problem and switch the power back on. And the technique of operating it was important, too. The gang's method seems to have been to cut the power, then quickly restore it. That way, staff were unable to find any obvious interruption to the supply and reported that power was flowing normally. The power would then be remotely cut again, and again, until there was no choice but to call the match off.

At least two games during 1997 were hit – West Ham v Crystal Palace and Wimbledon v Arsenal. On 3 November, West Ham had just equalised at 2-2 in the 65th minute when the lights went out. Electricians fought to bring them back on for half-an-hour – and they did briefly flicker into life – but they died again and the match was abandoned. West Ham's managing director Peter Storrie said, 'The floodlights contracted a fault which was impossible to find in the timescale.'

At Wimbledon, on 22 December, with the match only 13 seconds into the second half and the underdogs holding the mighty Arsenal 0-0, the lights were cut. Electricians worked on the fault for 12 minutes when suddenly the lights came back up. The teams warmed up on the pitch ready for the restart, only to be plunged into darkness again. The match was abandoned. Wimbledon director Sam Hammam clearly smelled a rat. There was already suspicion about the regularity of floodlight failures. 'Unless we stop this there will be shame on the game,' he said.

Stopped it finally was, when detectives swooped on three Malaysians and the head of security at Charlton Athletic's ground two days before the South London club faced Liverpool on 13 February 1999. The gang had got into the power room and installed their device, which an official later said 'had a lot of wires coming out of it and could be activated by remote control'. One gang member had a ticket for the game. Police found a remote control in the men's car.

Their downfall was roping in the security chief. He had been promised £20,000 for getting the crooks in. But he, in turn, tried to bribe a member of his staff with £5,000 to turn a blind eye – and that man tipped off police.

Chee Kew Ong and Eng Hwa Lim went to jail for four years. Ong admitted being behind the two abandoned games in 1997. An accomplice, Wai Yuen Liu, got 2.5 years. Crooked guard Roger Firth got one-and-a-half.

Judge Fabyan Evans told them, 'People derive much pleasure from following professional sport. Any interference from criminal organisations causes great offence and annoyance.'

SERIE A's BUSINESS
The Shame of Italian Football

To say Italian football experienced highs and lows in the summer of 2006 would be a hilarious understatement. At the very moment it won the World Cup for the fourth time, the nation was reeling from a match-fixing scandal involving four of its top clubs. Thirteen of the twenty-three stars in the Italian squad played for these sides – even as they lifted the trophy they knew they would probably have to find new employers.

The corruption – clubs influencing referees and linesmen to get favourable decisions – was unearthed by police probing an entirely different allegation. Back in 1998, Zdenek Zeman, former coach of Italian teams Lazio and Roma, claimed doping was rife in Serie A, the country's equivalent of England's Premiership. Only steroids, he said, could explain the physical bulk of certain top players from Juventus, Italy's most successful club.

Police tapped the phones of executives from the Turin giants and, from the thousands of calls, uncovered murky links between them and referees.

The case was not solid enough for criminal charges, but it was obviously against the sport's rules and the tapes were handed to the Italian Football Federation. The press got hold of them and published them in May 2006.

They made astonishing reading. Luciano Moggi, general manager of Juventus, had frequent conversations with Pierluigi Pairetto, who, as head of Italy's referees, picked officials for matches. Moggi was heard lobbying Pairetto for officials favourable to Juventus, and vetoing those he didn't like.

After a German ref disallowed a Juventus goal in a Champions League qualifier, Moggi allegedly demanded, 'What kind of referee did you send us?' Then he added, 'I have to make the return match in Stockholm secure, no?'

Damningly, Pairetto was heard in another tapped phone conversation advising a referee about to take charge of a Juventus game, 'You know what you have to do. Make sure you see everything. Even that which isn't there.'

Other big clubs – AC Milan, Fiorentina and Lazio – were implicated, too. Bosses at Fiorentina and Lazio were said to have asked Moggi to wield his influence on their behalf as they fought relegation in 2004/05. Milan were accused of trying to secure 'favourable' refs and linesmen for their games, too.

Moggi and the Juventus board resigned en masse a few days after the scandal became public. Nineteen games were investigated as suspicious and a host of club executives and match officials were charged by prosecutors on behalf of the Italian Football Federation. In the end, 24 were kicked out of the sport.

Moggi was fined £35,000 and banned for five years. Juventus chief executive Antonio Giraudo was fined £14,000 and banned for five years. Referees' chief Pairetto was banned for two-and-a-half years. AC Milan vice-president Adriano Galliani was banned for a year.

Initially, the most damaging punishments were handed down to the clubs themselves. Juventus were relegated to the second division (Serie B) with a 30-point handicap. They were stripped of their last two league titles and barred from the Champions League.

Lazio were relegated to Serie B with a seven-point deduction. Florence-based Fiorentina were relegated with a 12-point penalty. AC Milan stayed in Serie A but were barred from European competition for a season and handed a 15-point penalty.

The football world applauded such draconian punishments as a suitable deterrent. But the scandal then descended into farce. On appeal, Fiorentina and Lazio were reinstated to Serie A, with Fiorentina deducted 19 points and Lazio 11. Fiorentina's penalty was then cut to 15 points and Lazio's to only 3. AC Milan's was cut from 15 to 8 and they were reinstated in the Champions League, which they went on to win in May 2007. Juventus's original handicap, 30 points, was cut to 17 as the season began and then to just 9. Despite having to sell six superstar players as a result of their relegation, they were on top of Serie B within weeks and remained there during 2006-7, winning promotion back to Serie A in just one season.

Zeman, the coach who triggered the scandal, summed up the contempt many felt for such a U-turn. 'Football has lost a wonderful opportunity to clean up its act,' he said. 'It may never come again if this is the way even cases as serious as these are going to be fudged in future. The entire system is rotten and should have been punished.'

Chapter 4

Druggies

SUSPECT DEVICE
Michel Pollentier

There have been many ruses to cheat a drug test.
Cyclist Michel Pollentier dreamed up probably the
most inventive and, as it turned out, the most
blatant. Not for him the subtle masking agents
others might have deployed to conceal any
performance-enhancing substance. Not for him
tampering with the test, or dodging it completely.
His subterfuge was a contraption worthy of
Professor Branestawm. It comprised a small rubber
bulb suitable for containing liquid, connected to a
tube. Squeezing the bulb would propel liquid
down the tube and out of the other end.

Pollentier, then 27, was no slouch as a cyclist. Far from it. The diminutive, balding Belgian was an international athlete of great repute. During one golden year, 1977, he won the Tour of Italy, led the Tour of Switzerland from start to finish and won the Belgian Road Race Championship. Earlier, in a time trial, he beat his seemingly invincible compatriot Eddy Merckx – still arguably history's greatest cyclist.

Pollentier was at his peak at the start of the Tour de France in 1978. He took the coveted yellow jersey as race leader after a stunning victory on the race's most famous mountain climb, the Alpe d'Huez in the French Alps. Just two hours after finishing, his race and his career were in tatters.

Word had spread among the competitors that, despite the Tour's notorious reputation for doping, that year's drug testers were being particularly slapdash and 'flexible' in their approach. At the time, it was thought common practice for competitors to avoid detection by substituting their real urine for an untainted sample. Pollentier, perhaps confident in the testers' laxity, retired to his room to rig up his bulb-and-tube device, which he hid under his jersey. The bulb, full of drug-free urine from an unknown source, was held in his armpit. Pollentier ran its plastic connecting pipe down his torso and taped it to his penis. The idea was that when handed a specimen flask, he would pump the bulb with his arm, like a bagpipe-player, and the untainted urine would flow down the pipe and out into the test tube.

Pollentier showed up for the test unaware that on duty was a rookie tester determined, on his first job, to play everything by the book. The official demanded that Pollentier and two others provide their specimens in his full view, with their trousers and underpants down and jerseys pulled up. The first cyclist lifted his jersey to reveal a contraption just like Pollentier's. Within moments, Pollentier was busted, too.

The Belgian attempted an excuse – that he had wet himself with the effort of the gruelling mountain stage and had insufficient urine left for the test, so had to find a way round it.

There was no mercy. He was kicked out of the Tour and suspended for two months. The Belgian returned to the sport, achieving decent results – but the drug test fiasco hung over him for the rest of his career. He retired in 1984 and opened a garage.

KING OF CHEATS
Ben Johnson

Ben Johnson has gone down in history as the king of all sports cheats. He was the man who, in 46 strides, trounced his rivals in the biggest event of the 1988 Seoul Olympics – the 100 metres – casually smashing the world record and exuding superhuman self-belief to match superhuman athleticism. Within two days, the Jamaican-born Canadian was exposed as a steroid user and stripped of his gold and his record.

The seeds of Johnson's disgrace were sewn seven years before the great race for which he will for ever be infamous. He was just 19 back in September 1981 when his coach Charlie Francis took him to one side and made a suggestion that would shape both their lives. Francis said steroids could give Johnson an extra 1 per cent on the track. That's worth a metre over 100 metres – possibly the difference between Olympic gold and fourth place.

Johnson – young, naïve and not especially educated – agreed.

That year, he was ranked outside the world's top ten 100-metre sprinters. The world number one was Carl Lewis and, for five years, the American was untouchable. Johnson was barely on his radar by the time of the Los Angeles Olympics in 1984, although the Canadian had steadily climbed the rankings and was world number four. Lewis, who won four golds at the Games, later described him dismissively as 'one of the sprinters I didn't know much about... a Canadian'.

That unknown Canadian was fast enough to take bronze. By the next year, he was a serious challenger, even beating Lewis in one race. Lewis was still world number one, but Johnson was a close second. In 1986, those positions switched round as Johnson beat Lewis convincingly at a big event in Moscow.

The rivalry was bitter, and grew hostile at the 1987 World Championships in Rome. Johnson had now won all of their previous four races and broken the ten-second barrier three times that year, a feat Lewis could not yet match. In the final, Johnson stormed to victory in an astonishing world record of 9.83 seconds, with Lewis second at 9.93.

Lewis, not the world's greatest loser, threw around excuses, then accusations. He didn't mention Johnson's name, but he said, 'There are gold medallists at this meet who are on drugs. That race will be looked at for many years, for more reasons than one. There are a lot of people coming out of nowhere. I don't think they are doing it without drugs. I could run 9.8 or faster in the 100 if I could jump into drugs right away.'

Johnson dismissed this as sour grapes. 'When

Carl Lewis was winning everything, I never said a word against him,' he said. 'And when the next guy comes along and beats me, I won't complain about that either.'

There was more to their rivalry than mere jockeying for position as the world's best sprinter. Lewis was the educated, articulate, all-American golden boy, a supreme all-round athlete and proven winner. Johnson stuttered and was of moderate intellect, and his muscular bulk caused many to wonder whether he was on steroids.

By now, Johnson, a national hero in Canada and with money pouring in, was so dominant over Lewis that it threatened to make the 100 metres at Seoul a one-man race. But early in the year, Johnson was injured and Lewis came into great form.

With a month to go before the Olympics, Lewis won a 100 metres in Zurich, with Johnson back in third. 'The gold medal for the Olympic 100 metres is mine,' bragged Lewis, typically. 'I will never again lose to Johnson.'

Johnson returned home to Toronto, where, under Francis's guidance, he had injections of steroids and a growth hormone. He then had further treatment to remove traces of the steroids in time to dodge the scrutiny of the Olympic drug testers.

Johnson arrived in Seoul convinced of his supremacy over 100 metres, especially with the boost his steroids were giving him. After an almost disastrously casual run in the first round, from which he qualified only as a fastest loser, he won his semi-final. Lewis won the other. The stage was set for an epic showdown. 'I'm in the best shape I've ever been in,' Lewis said. 'Ben will have to run a perfect race to beat me. I don't think he can.'

But the truth was that Johnson knew he would win, and Lewis, consumed by the suspicion that his rival had an unfair advantage, probably knew he would win, too. Johnson said simply, 'When the gun goes off, the race be over.'

Johnson's race was perfect. It was astounding. He smashed the world record, in 9.79 seconds, despite coasting in the last two strides with his arm raised in triumph. Who knows what his time might have been had he finished at full pace? Lewis took silver and Britain's Linford Christie bronze.

For once, Lewis was measured in his reaction to defeat, saying only that he was happy with his own performance, a US record of 9.92 seconds. Years later, in his autobiography, he voiced his true feelings, alluding to the yellowness of Johnson's eyes, caused by steroid damage to his liver. 'I couldn't get away from those yellow eyes,' Lewis said. 'The bastard did it again.'

Johnson was naturally ecstatic, and fired with a

conviction that he was the greatest sprinter of all time,' something he still believes. He said, 'I think this record will last 50 years, maybe 100 years. If I had not eased off in the last two metres, it could have been 9.75. But I'll save that for another time.'

The euphoria lasted just two days. And what happened next is still argued over by the Johnson and Lewis camps two decades later. Johnson's urine sample taken after the race was found to contain the banned anabolic steroid stanozolol. The Canadian immediately insisted he was innocent and said someone, somehow, had spiked his sample with the drug.

His manager Larry Heiderbrecht told reporters, 'Ben is obviously sick at the news and will appeal. He is shattered. He does not take drugs. It is obvious that something very strange has been happening. Nobody is that stupid to take drugs a few days before a big race. It would appear that the stuff has been in his system for a short period of time.

'Ben makes a lot of money from the sport and there is a lot of financial incentive for someone to do something. His training bag could have been left unattended and somebody could have interfered with it. The whole of Canada has been on his back but that would not make him take drugs.'

Heiderbrecht even claimed a mysterious official had given Johnson a soft drink during the championship which left a 'yellow, gooey' residue his doctor was suspicious of. 'I think Ben is a very trusting young man who put himself in a spot where perhaps he's created a lot of problems for himself,' said Heiderbrecht.

But the International Olympic Committee rejected the claims and stripped Johnson of his gold and his world record. As Lewis's silver was upgraded to gold and Christie's bronze to silver, Johnson flew home in disgrace.

Johnson and his coach Francis admit that the athlete had been on steroids beforehand. But the drug regimes Francis organised for his athletes were very precise. Stanozolol is well known to take 28 days to clear the system, twice as long as other steroids. It seems odd that Francis would have mistimed the dose to expose Johnson to a positive test right after the final.

For his part, Johnson claims he knew nothing of the specific drug that nailed him. In a TV documentary in 2006, he said, 'I knew what I was taking, and I never came across that drug. I knew it was placed there.' Besides, he added, 'You cannot run that kind of time with that kind of drug. It makes you very stiff, very tight.'

Another sensational development gave the disgraced sprinter even more ammunition. A mystery man who had shared a beer with Johnson in the drug test waiting area turned out to be a friend of his deadliest rival, Lewis. Johnson claimed the man, a former American footballer named André Jackson, spiked his drink to ensure a positive test and hand Lewis the title. In 2006, he told a newspaper, 'I have the information on how it was done and why it was done this way and who was behind it.'

Lewis admits he knew Jackson, but rubbishes any suggestion that Johnson's beer was tampered with. Nonetheless, it was remarkable that, despite high security, Jackson – merely an athletics fan with no official accreditation – could have wandered into the drug testing area for an event as high-profile as the men's 100 metres. Lewis said, 'I'm not sure how André got in. Either he had one of my passes or admission to the area or he got one from an Olympic official. The passes were amazingly easy to get, considering how strict the overall security was.'

Lewis said he spoke to Jackson after providing his own urine sample, and asked him what he was doing there. Jackson said he was curious about the drug-testing area but also keen to watch Johnson's physio, in case he slipped the athlete a masking agent – a substance that hides drug traces in urine.

Lewis's manager Joe Douglas has since admitted that, in theory, he would place a spy in the testing area if he suspected a rival athlete was up to no good. Douglas said, 'If I thought Ben was going to take a masking agent, I might plant somebody in there to take a photo of it.' But he insisted, 'Carl had absolutely nothing to do with Ben testing positive.' Sabotage was also ruled out by the IOC and by the Canadian inquiry into the scandal.

The two-year ban Johnson received effectively ended his career. He made a comeback in January 1991 but never regained his world-beating form. At the 1992 Barcelona Olympics, he failed to make the 100 metres final, although he insists that the never-ending battery of drug tests he was put through destroyed his performance.

'I was making a great comeback, but I went out in the semi-finals because my federation sabotaged me,' Johnson said. 'They could not live with Ben Johnson making a great comeback. If I had come back and won the Olympic Games, I would have been bigger than the Olympics. They could not live with that, so somebody had to set me up again.

'I had been tested in every race I had run in Europe in 1991 and 1992 and everything was clear. I was running fast, running clean. They drug-tested me five times in the Olympic Village in one day because they knew I was in great shape and they didn't want me to win the Olympics again. It would have been embarrassing for the IAAF, the

IOC and maybe my federation. They drug-tested me the day before the race and I didn't get to bed until the morning of my first round at 9.30am. I got through two rounds but the next day I could not hold on because my body had not recovered from two days earlier. They used up all my energy and it affected my performance.'

The end finally came in January 1993 when Johnson tested positive for steroids again at an athletics meeting in Montreal. This time he was banned for life by the International Association of Athletics Federations.

Johnson still insists he was clean at Seoul. He claims he is the greatest sprinter in history and would have beaten every other world or Olympic champion since. 'If you put Donovan Bailey, Maurice Greene and Tim Montgomery in my race in Seoul, they would finish behind me,' he said. 'It was the greatest race ever run. Every ten-metre segment was perfect, all the way down the track.

'I could have run 9.72 if I had not shut down at 94 metres. And track surfaces now are a lot faster than I was using. I don't watch the sport any more. It's a waste of time. Nobody impresses me. Nobody can run like Ben Johnson.

'Regardless of what I did, I am still the best sprinter of all time. Most people loved the entertainment and know the game. The sport will never be clean. It's going to be going on until the end of time.'

In hindsight, the 1988 men's 100 metres final at the Seoul Olympics proved to be the dirtiest race in history. Of the eight finishers, five tested positive for drugs either before or after the race itself. Here they are, with their original placings in the race before Johnson's disqualification:

1. Ben Johnson

The Canadian was disqualified and sent home in shame from the Games.

2. Carl Lewis

Fifteen years after the race, it was revealed that the American golden boy could have been banned from the 1988 Games for taking banned stimulants. Dr Wade Exum, ex-director of drug control for the US Olympic Committee, said Lewis – who made holier-than-thou speeches against drug cheats – failed three tests at the US trials before Seoul. Lewis's claim, that the stimulants were contained in a herbal supplement he took in all innocence, was accepted by authorities and the tests covered up. It has been argued that a winner of four golds at the previous Olympics should have known at all times what he was putting in his body.

3. Linford Christie

Britain's greatest sprinter failed a test for the stimulant ephedrine at the Seoul Games. By a slender margin, the International Olympic Committee voted to accept his claim that it was the result of ginseng tea he had drunk. Christie, who went on to win 100 metres gold at the 1992 Olympics, was in semi-retirement by 1999 when he tested positive for the banned steroid nandrolone. That earned him a two-year ban.

5. Dennis Mitchell

The American was banned for two years in 1998 after testing positive for excessive testosterone. His excuse – that he had 'five bottles of beer and sex with his wife at least four times' the night before the test – was thrown out by athletics chiefs.

7. Desai Williams

Johnson's Canadian stablemate admitted using steroids during the Canadian Government's 1989 inquiry into performance-enhancing drugs in athletics.

DECEIT OF A NATION
East Germany's Drug Programme

During the Cold War Communist East Germany was determined to flex its muscles on the world stage at any price, especially at sport. But those manly biceps often belonged to women, a generation of world-beating freaks manufactured by a sinister, top-secret, State-run programme of drug cheating.

For two decades, the world watched with open suspicion as a comparatively small nation of 17 million began punching well above its weight at the Olympic Games and World Championships.

Within one four-year period, it doubled its tally of Olympic golds from 20 to 40. For sporting glory, it ranked alongside the superpowers of the United States and the Soviet Union.

But no one watching an Olympics in the 1970s and 1980s – let alone competing in one – had any doubt that something dodgy was afoot. Many of East Germany's huge female athletes were indistinguishable from men. When one American swimmer remarked on her rivals' deep voices, their coach retorted, 'We are here to swim, not to sing.'

The truth was that the Government was pumping 10,000 athletes full of dangerous, performance-boosting steroids. Some were given injections or pills from the age of 11. They had no idea what the mysterious drugs were – their cynical coaches told them they were vitamins 'for your own good'.

The programme, named State Plan 14.25, was the brainchild of Dr Manfred Hoeppner, East Germany's chief medical officer, who recommended it to his Government in 1968. The country's sports minister and Olympic chief Manfred Ewald, a former Nazi, ran it enthusiastically.

Hundreds of scientists and doctors were ordered to research and create the illegal drugs, plus masking agents to hide traces of them during testing.

Gold medals and world records quickly flowed, particularly among the swimmers. At the Munich Olympics in 1972, East Germany won more golds than its arch-rival West Germany. In 1976, it doubled its gold tally to 40, winning 11 of the 13 women's swimming events.

One strapping lass from Leipzig, 6ft 1in Kristin Otto, won an astonishing six golds at the 1988 Seoul Olympics and was unanimously voted the outstanding athlete of the Games by the International Olympic Committee. Six years later, after the fall of the Berlin Wall and the examination of files once kept hidden by the Stasi secret police, her drug use, and that of many other top East German athletes, was exposed.

Otto had testosterone levels in 1989 three times greater than the minimum needed to trigger a positive test result. Her amazing record suddenly counted for nothing.

Phillip Whitton, editor of a US swimming magazine that published the results, said, 'She had more testosterone in her than the entire starting team of the Dallas Cowboys. No wonder she won six golds.'

The East German mass-doping programme – combined with the strategy of 'hot-housing' promising kids in specialist academies from a very early age – produced young teenagers capable of smashing world records.

But the long-term health consequences were dire. Women's breasts shrunk, their voices deepened, they were prone to infertility, miscarriages, deformed babies, excessive hair, liver failure, cancer and mental problems.

A shot-putter named Heidi Krieger, European champion in 1986, blamed the pills when she later changed sex and became Andreas. The swimmer Carola Nitschke – world record-holder at 14 and European champion at 15 – was so ashamed when the truth emerged that she returned her medals and demanded her achievements be struck from the record. She had been given testosterone injections at 13 and was taking 30 pills a day. 'Without the pharmaceuticals, I wouldn't have been in the world's top swimmers,' she bluntly admitted.

In the late 1990s, a string of other swimmers came forward to denounce their doctors and coaches. But the Stasi had destroyed many of the most incriminating files. So, of the hundreds of authority figures in on the plot, only Ewald and Hoeppner faced the music. In 2000, they were found guilty of systematically doping hundreds of athletes, but amazingly escaped with suspended jail terms despite the catalogue of misery they inflicted on thousands of people.

Dr Warner Franke, a German biochemist who investigated the Stasi files, concluded, 'Without a doubt, every single world-class East German athlete was doped.'

LABORATORY RATS
The BALCO Controversy

Sport's biggest drugs scandal since the Ben Johnson affair exposed a string of high-profile cheats for the sneakiest of tricks – taking a steroid that no test could detect. British sprint ace Dwain Chambers made the headlines in the UK. In America, the scalps were far more significant – Tim Montgomery, the 100 metres world record holder, and Barry Bonds, baseball's biggest hitter and one of its all-time greats.

It exploded in 2003 when American athletics coach Trevor Graham told the United States Anti-Doping Agency that several track and field stars were using a new 'designer' steroid, Tetrahydrogestrinone. The drug, known as THG, had been altered by chemists to evade existing tests. Graham claimed a San Francisco food supplements firm, BALCO (Bay Area Laboratory Co-Operative), was distributing it.

Graham delivered to USADA a syringe containing THG, and scientists quickly developed a test for it. More than 500 old samples from athletes were retested and 20 were positive for THG.

A list of BALCO customers unearthed in a

subsequent raid on the firm's headquarters included Montgomery and Bonds.

Tests for THG later that year implicated Chambers, Britain's great sprint hope, who was European champion over 100 metres and joint holder of the European record. Chambers declared his innocence. He said that after he began training in the US in 2002, his coach introduced him to BALCO boss Victor Conte, a nutritionist who supplied him with what he thought was a diet supplement. 'I took THG, but I didn't know what its gains and benefits were,' Chambers insisted. 'It came in liquid form and you put a few drops under your tongue three to four times a week. I was a bit suspicious about why you would put it under your tongue, but Victor explained it was a new product that would aid me nutritionally, so I went forward with it.

'Nutrition wasn't something I was interested in, so when he was explaining all this scientific jargon to me about THG and various other supplements, it came in one ear and fell out of the other. In hindsight, I was very foolish not to ask certain questions about THG, but no one had ever heard of it before so I didn't see any reason to question it.'

Chambers was banned from athletics for two years. And he and his innocent relay team-mates

Christian Malcolm, Darren Campbell and Marlon Devonish were stripped of their silver medals from the 4x100 metres at the 2003 World Championships.

Montgomery, once the fastest man on Earth with a world record of 9.78 seconds in the 100 metres, never actually failed a drug test. But under questioning by a Grand Jury, he admitted Conte slipped him 'the clear', a code-name for THG, over eight months in 2001. He was banned from the track for two years in 2005 and promptly retired.

Meanwhile, Bonds – second on the all-time list of baseball's home run hitters – told the Grand Jury he unwittingly used two BALCO steroids – 'the cream' and 'the clear' – thinking they were flaxseed oil and a balm for arthritis. But an explosive book later alleged he had systematically used steroids since 1998 – and in early 2007 he was under investigation for perjury.

Various other track and field stars, American footballers and baseball players were implicated. Among them was Kelli White, a Californian sprinter who won gold in both the 100 and 200 metres at the World Championships in Paris in 2003. Although she did not fail a test for THG, she admitted using it – and lost every title she had won since 2000, plus more than £60,000 in prize money and £250,000 in endorsements. 'I have not only cheated myself, but also my family, friends and sport,' she said.

The men behind the BALCO scandal, Conte and two accomplices, all went to jail.

SPEED FREAK
Justin Gatlin

When the Olympic and world 100-metre sprint champion Justin Gatlin was busted for his second drugs offence, there were few of the screaming headlines that trumpeted Ben Johnson's fall from grace in the 1980s. So regularly were top-class athletes now found guilty of doping offences that Gatlin's positive test for a banned substance was greeted with a world-weary sigh. But the story really livened up thanks to his coach's fantastic explanation – Gatlin had been framed by a shifty masseur who rubbed an illicit drug-laced lotion into his legs.

Gatlin, born in Brooklyn, New York, and raised in Florida, was a sensational runner, one of the all-time greats. Originally a 110-metre hurdler, he converted into a sprinter, but a positive drug test for amphetamines in 2001 knocked his career sideways early on. He got a two-year suspension, though it was quickly lifted when he persuaded authorities that the substance was contained in the medicine he took for attention deficit disorder, a condition he was diagnosed with as a child.

Gatlin went from strength to strength, winning gold at the Athens Olympics in 2004, then the world title the following year. Athletics legend Michael Johnson agreed he was 'the best sprinter in the world'. In May 2006, Gatlin equalled the 100 metres world record of 9.77 seconds, set by Jamaica's Asafa Powell in 2005. He was still only 24 – and it was felt even greater things lay ahead. Tempting fate, he said, 'I feel kinda blessed. I have to give thanks to God that I've always been steered down the right path.'

But his destruction was already under way. A drug test taken at a minor race in Kansas City a month before his world record came back positive for excessive testosterone. It was his second offence – and would normally carry a life ban. Gatlin was told the result in June and went public with it a month later. 'I have been informed that, after a relay race I ran in Kansas City on 22 April, I tested positive for "testosterone or its precursors,"' he said. 'I cannot account for these results, because I have never knowingly used any banned substance or authorised anyone to administer such a substance to me. Since learning of the positive test, I have been doing everything in my power to find out what caused this to happen. I hope that when all the facts are revealed it will be determined that I have done nothing wrong.'

Referring to his first positive test in 2001 he added, 'That experience made me even more vigilant to make certain that I do not come into contact with any banned substance for any reason whatsoever, because any additional anti-doping rule offence could mean a lifetime ban from the sport that I love. Since the positive test at the University of Tennessee, I have been involved with efforts to educate people about the dangers of using drugs and would never do anything to disappoint my fans and supporters. It is simply not consistent with either my character or my confidence in my God-given athletic ability to cheat in any way.'

The head of US athletics, Craig Masback, said, 'USA Track & Field is gravely concerned that Justin Gatlin has tested positive for banned substances. We hope Justin has not committed a doping offence, and we await the completion of the adjudication process.'

Then Gatlin's controversial coach Trevor Graham, weighed in. He sensationally claimed that an unnamed massage therapist rubbed testosterone cream into Gatlin's legs without the runner's knowledge.

'We know the person who did this,' Graham said. 'Justin is devastated. Myself, too. We're extremely upset right now. We are trying to go out and make sure we can prove his innocence, and we hope this individual has the guts to come forward and say he did it.'

The masseur was found and denied everything. And even Gatlin's legal team wanted nothing to do with the bizarre allegation. His lawyer Cameron Myler said, 'Trevor's comments were not made with the knowledge or authorisation of either Justin or us.'

The International Association of Athletics Federations said claims of sabotage would carry no weight anyway. 'Whatever is found in an athlete's body when tested is his or her responsibility,' said a spokesman. 'We have been advising athletes for years of the strict liability policy and encouraged them to be very cautious when receiving any form of treatment.'

Gatlin co-operated fully with the authorities, and the lifetime ban he could have been given on the two-strikes-and-you're-out rule was reduced to eight years. The 'exceptional circumstances' of his positive drug test in 2001 were also considered mitigating factors. He was stripped of his joint world record, but that was it. An eight-year ban would effectively end the career of a 24-year-old sprinter. But the deal Gatlin struck with the US Anti-Doping Agency allowed him to appeal to get the ban reduced further. This has yet to be heard at the time of going to press.

Gatlin said, 'I have put my faith in a system that I believe will clear my name and that I believe will allow me to compete again. Cheating, in any form, is completely contrary to who I am as an athlete and a person.'

In December 2006, while awaiting his appeal, Gatlin had a secret trial with American football team the Houston Texans. He was pondering a new career as a wide receiver. Texans coach Gary Kubiak said, 'Some of our people were amazed at how fast he ran – and he can certainly catch the ball pretty good.' In May 2007, Gatlin was also being considered as a potential wide receiver by the Tampa Bay Buccaneers NFL team.

DRUG PEDALLER
Floyd Landis

It was perhaps the most astonishing ride in the history of cycling. Floyd Landis, down and out of the 2006 Tour de France and needing a hip replacement, destroyed the field on the 17th stage with seemingly superhuman physical and mental strength. On and on he rode through the Alps for 124 gruelling miles, 74 of them toiling alone, up front, as his incredulous rivals watched him disappear into the distance. A few days later he won the entire Tour. In May 2007, Gatlin was also being considered as a potential wide receiver by the Tampa Bay Buccaneers NFL team.

But perhaps Landis was not quite the superman he seemed. A Mennonite from Lancaster County, Pennsylvania, Landis had at one stage held the yellow jersey given to the leader of the Tour – a 2,261-mile race held over 20 different stages and time trials throughout France.

But on the 16th stage he finished a disastrous 23rd, way behind the winner, and had to concede the overall lead. His form seemed shot. All hope seemed lost. No one gave him a prayer of recovering the top spot.

Then came a moment of absolute supremacy, the epic ride from St-Jean-de-Maurienne to Morzine on Thursday 20 July, a stage involving five punishing climbs. Landis attacked his rivals on the first one, took the lead and continued his lone breakaway for 74 miles. Only one cyclist kept up with him, and even he was left trailing in Landis's wake at the foot of the last climb. 'Floyd was like a motorbike. He was unbelievable,' said an Australian rider, Michael Rogers.

Landis won the stage by five minutes and four seconds, and was now just 30 seconds overall behind Tour leader Oscar Pereiro - who admitted, 'I couldn't do much about Floyd today. He did an amazing ride, full stop.'

The co-director of Landis's team, Juan Fernandez, said, 'Floyd was like an injured lion who needed to restore his wounded pride by striking out at whatever cost. And it worked.'

After solid performances in the following two stages and a solo time trial, Landis won the Tour de France, cycling triumphantly into the Champs-Elysées in Paris, where 250,000 people greeted him, the American flag was raised and the strains of the 'Star-Spangled Banner' rang out. Landis had won the great race for America for the eighth year running, following Lance Armstrong's seven victories.

And then it all fell apart.

Four days later came the announcement that Landis had tested positive for an illegally high level of testosterone in his urine sample at the end of his extraordinary ride on Stage 17. It was 11 times higher than the average man's. He was sacked by his team, his £300,000 winnings were withheld and he looked likely to be stripped of his title.

Landis denied taking banned substances, variously blaming thyroid medicine, painkilling injections for his bad hip, naturally high testosterone production and even a whisky he drank the night before Stage 17.

But his lawyers turned their attention to the tests themselves, claiming they were unreliable and that the French laboratory mislabelled his samples anyway.

Landis said, 'I don't fault people for believing I must be guilty. If I were looking in from the outside, I'd be feeling exactly the same way. But I'd like to be given a fair trial and the evidence to be considered with an open mind.'

He believed the most compelling evidence in his favour was the cast-iron certainty of being drug-tested and, if guilty, caught, after winning a stage of the Tour. 'The chances of me getting away with it would be zero,' he said. 'And even if I had taken that course, would I then be so useless in the press conference and so devoid of explanation? Wouldn't I have my defence all worked out? This must make me the dumbest person on the whole planet. The accusation, in reality, is that I'm an idiot.'

There was widespread scepticism. Pat McQuaid, president of the International Cycling Union, said, 'Every athlete who tests positive blames the system and somebody else. Floyd's no different.'

Landis has written a book, *Positively False*, outlining his defence. He faced the US Anti-

Doping Agency in May 2007. The decision on whether to ban him and strip him of his title was pending as this book went to press.

DEEP TROUBLE
Michelle Smith

The red-haired Irish swimmer Michelle Smith became a worldwide superstar at the 1996 Atlanta Olympics, winning three golds and a bronze. Nicole Kidman was said to be lined up to play her in a blockbuster movie. But Smith's sudden rise from journeyman to world-beater aroused enormous suspicion, especially among her defeated American rivals. When a random drug test two years later was mysteriously contaminated with whisky, she was subsequently banned from the sport whilst continuing to protest her innocence. She has kept her medals because there has never been any evidence to suggest that she used illegal substances.

In the two previous Olympics, Smith's best placing was 17th, in the 200-metre backstroke. In 1993, she was ranked world number 90 in the 400-metre individual medley.

But that year she began training with her future husband Erik de Bruin, a former Dutch discus thrower serving a four-year suspension for failing a drug test. After that, her progress was incredible.

Within a year, Smith jumped to world number 17 in the 400 metres. While her time had improved by just 5.32 seconds in the four years up to 1992, it improved by 17.27 seconds in less than two years before Atlanta – an astonishing achievement at 26 years of age.

She came fifth in the 200 metres butterfly at the 1994 World Championships and, the following year, set Irish records in nine events, also picking up two European titles.

Smith put her new-found success down to nothing other than hard graft. 'I train six days a week, six hours a day,' she said. 'All I do is eat, sleep and train. If you looked at a photograph of how I was four years ago, you would see these big fat cheeks. Now I'm an awful lot leaner.'

In Atlanta, Smith won gold in the 400 metres individual medley, 400 metres freestyle and 200 metres individual medley, plus bronze in the 200 metres butterfly. It was Ireland's second-largest Olympic medal haul in history, and she was solely responsible.

Smith passed five drug tests at the Games. The Americans were dismissed as sore losers, and Smith came out fighting. 'I'm not going to be stupid enough once I've reached the top to take drugs,' Smith asserted. 'I am clean. I repeat – I don't cheat. I train by swimming 100km a week. I eat the right things. My coach and husband Erik de Bruin has given me great advice and training.'

De Bruin added, 'Her success is down to determination, nothing else. Nobody in that pool has worked as hard.'

Plenty were on her side. Bill Clinton, then US President, posed alongside her. She was courted by Hollywood producers keen to film a humble Irish girl's sporting triumph over adversity. One agent claimed Nicole Kidman would play her and Tom Cruise her husband.

Smith did innumerable interviews, appeared on TV's *A Question of Sport*, made television adverts and went to a movie première alongside its star Liam Neeson. A Dublin band recorded a version of the Beatles hit 'Michelle' in her honour.

In the pool, there was now no stopping her as she picked up two golds and two silvers at the 1997 European Championships in Seville. The drug allegations, she said, had strengthened her resolve. 'I have had my detractors, but I try to use all that to my advantage,' she said. 'I have proven again this week that I am one of the top swimmers and I have done myself proud.' But she added, 'It is so upsetting and hurtful to stand on the podium receiving a medal for Ireland and think people still doubt me.'

Early one morning in January 1998, FINA drug testers arrived at Smith and de Bruin's home in County Kilkenny demanding a urine sample. Even before they left, they thought they could smell alcohol in it.

Tests at a laboratory in Barcelona approved by the International Olympic Committee confirmed the presence of a huge amount of whisky. The proportion of alcohol in the sample would have been fatal for any human.

The testers said that only Smith could have doctored it – she had been alone with the sample for five minutes. FINA agreed, banning Smith for four years, effectively ending her career. FINA chief Gunnar Werner was quick to condemn her. 'Manipulation is a bad crime,' he said. 'It is more or less two abuses in one – interfering with a sample to cover up something else.'

Smith lost a subsequent appeal at the Court of Arbitration for Sport. But ironically, her battle there sparked an interest in law, which she went on to study, becoming a barrister in 2005.

Chapter 5

Imposters

FIT AS A FIDDLE
The Bogus Paralympians

Morally, it doesn't get worse than cheating disabled athletes out of medals – but that's precisely what a Spanish basketball team did, because almost all of them were faking their disabilities.

The Sydney Paralympics of 2000 was a prestige event that saw 136 countries competing in the fabulous stadia used for the full Olympics that year. A glittering opening ceremony saw Kylie Minogue sing 'Waltzing Matilda' and the disco classic 'Celebration'.

The Spanish contingent was scandal-prone that year. It turned out, for example, that its top disabled swimmer, Sebastian Rodriguez – eventual winner of five golds – had not lost the use of his legs in a car crash, as he claimed. In fact, he had a dark secret – he was a convicted terrorist and murderer left handicapped after a long hunger-strike in jail.

At least he was genuinely disabled. That's more than could be said of about ten of the twelve players in the Spanish basketball team that entered the tournament for the mentally, as opposed to physically, handicapped.

Plainly, a mental disability is harder to measure than a physical one, it being invisible. So a benchmark was set at an IQ level of 75. Below that, you qualified; above it, you didn't. But several countries, not just Spain, were lax in keeping records of their players' IQ tests. And the organisers of the Paralympics seem to have taken it on trust that the players were as mentally impaired as they claimed.

It was a grey area and the Spaniards capitalised on it when they couldn't find enough players scoring below 75 to make up the team. By 1998, they had only two and began casting around for more. Journalist Carlos Ribagorda, 26, smelled a story and joined the team, undercover, posing as a mentally handicapped man.

One might expect to be asked for documents proving one's limited IQ in order to qualify for a team vying for medals on the world stage. Ribagorda wasn't. He was merely asked for six sit-ups and a blood pressure test. Once he'd obliged, he was in. 'There were no real checks, no examination of medical records,' he said. 'I just went along and told them I suffered from being mentally handicapped. I was soon practising with the squad and on my way to Sydney.'

The journalist quickly discovered he wasn't the only player in the side with a perfectly normal IQ – they seemed to be the overwhelming majority. Indeed, the Spanish basketball magazine *Gigantes* later claimed that many players had shown up from ordinary amateur clubs. Another was even said to be a professional.

Any team of mentally able basketballers will have distinct advantages over those with IQs under 75 – greater tactical awareness and faster reactions chief among them. And so it proved as the tournament got under way. The Spaniards' obvious superiority aroused the suspicion of other teams and journalists. At one point, Ribagorda said, the coach told them they were playing too well and ordered them to slow their scoring down.

Spanish journalists began to sniff a scandal – so the coach told the athletes to grow beards and wear hats to avoid being recognised so easily back home if their photos were published.

Brendan Flynn, head of the Australian Paralympics Committee, knew something was afoot. He said some of the Spanish players were talented enough to play in Australia's National Basketball League.

The Spaniards duly reached the final, against Russia, triumphing by 87 points to 63 and taking gold. Russia's coach Igor Kopylov had his own suspicions, but not enough to protest officially. 'After the competition, there were no protests from anyone,' he said. 'But we suspected some discrepancy with the members of the Spanish team. Tactically, they were much better than us, which can only suggest one thing – they had good mental capacity.'

Then Ribagorda broke his story. The scandal was front-page news around the world. He and his team-mates were ordered to hand back their medals, and the title was given to the Russians. Three top Spanish Paralympics officials quit.

Ribagorda said, 'It did not make me feel very good about myself to be out there playing, knowing that I was OK and that nearly everyone else in the team was, too. But there can be no cheating, and that's why I wrote the exposé.'

The furore cast doubt over the credibility of the entire Paralympic movement. The International

Paralympic Committee investigated and found only a third of the 244 mentally handicapped athletes at Sydney had the necessary documents to prove their eligibility. IPC chief Thomas Reinecke said, 'It is a concern that the areas where most forms were not filled out was in the name and signature of the person who was supposed to determine the athlete's IQ. It is then that you have to question whether they were disabled.'

He added that all 25 of the forms sent in by Spain's Paralympics committee were incomplete and that some former Soviet countries had also used 'the Spanish system', which he described by saying, 'You need between 12 and 15 players to fill a basketball team. Some of these countries just did not have 12 or 15 eligible players, so just found extras to fill the team.'

The scandal triggered a draconian ban on all intellectually-challenged athletes competing at the Paralympics, which, by 2007, was still in force and likely to remain so. Having had its fingers burned in 2000, the IPC seemed reluctant to trust any system of verifying an athlete's mental handicap.

So, finally, the big question – why did the athletes do it? Top British Paralympian Tanni Grey-Thompson, who won four golds on the track at Sydney, explained, 'The same reason people take drugs. It's cheating to win a medal because of everything that brings – lottery support, other financial support and a fair amount of newspaper and TV coverage. You can get quite a lot of reward, financial or personal. It's a bizarre sign of how important success at the Paralympics has become, but it needs to be taken extremely seriously. There needs to be severe penalties.'

HIDDEN AGENDER
Stella Walsh

The sprinter Stella Walsh was an outstanding athlete in more ways than one. She held twelve world records and won two Olympic medals. But if one particularly outstanding feature of her anatomy had been discovered during her lifetime, she would never have competed as a woman at all.

Walsh was born Stanislawa Walasiewiczowna on 3 April 1911 in Poland, and moved to Cleveland, Ohio, as a baby. At school, she developed into a fine all-round athlete and, by her late teens, was winning American national championships, despite her Polish citizenship. She was the first woman to run the 100-yard dash in under 11 seconds, in a time of 10.8 seconds. Two years later, representing Poland at the 1932

Olympics in Los Angeles, she won gold in the 100 metres, equalling the world record in the process, while also finishing a creditable sixth in the discus.

Walsh ran the 200 metres in 23.6 seconds in 1935, a world record that stood for 17 years. She later broke the world long-jump record with a distance of 6.04 metres or 19ft 9.75in.

At Adolf Hitler's Olympics – Berlin, 1936 – Walsh finished second, losing her 100 metres crown to an American, Helen Stephens. Walsh's Polish supporters insisted Stephens was too fast to be a woman and lobbied for her to be medically examined. German doctors carried out the check – and confirmed that Stephens was a woman. Which is more than could be said of Walsh. But it took another 44 years before that became apparent.

On 4 December 1980, long after Walsh had retired and had been inducted into the US Track and Field Hall of Fame, she was walking across the car park of a Cleveland shopping centre when she was killed by a stray bullet fired during an armed robbery. A post mortem revealed the secret Walsh carried with her all of her 69 years – she was a man, with male genitals and both male and female chromosomes – a condition known as mosaicism.

The astonishing discovery sparked calls for her records and victories to be struck from the record. In the end, neither the bosses of the Olympics or of world athletics took any action.

BLADE RUNNER
Abbes Tehami

Algerian athlete Abbes Tehami underwent an amazing physical transformation while running to victory in the Brussels marathon – he grew taller and had time to shave his moustache off.

Well, that's one explanation. The reality, of course, is that the man who started the 1991 race in the number 62 vest wasn't the same man who finished it.

Crafty Tehami got his short, moustachioed trainer Bensalem Hamiani to run the first seven-and-a-half miles for him in a ruse to make sure of bagging the £4,000 prize.

Then Hamiani dashed off the course and into woods where Tehami was waiting to swap vests.

The race organiser Milou Blavier noticed Hamiani tiring before he 'dropped out' and disappeared into the trees. Imagine his surprise when seemingly the same athlete sprinted back on to the course and caught up with the leaders just three miles later. 'I said, "Gee, this is some comeback,"' Blavier said later.

Tehami, not at all a bad runner, won the race four minutes ahead of his rivals. But the hoax was so obvious that the crowd were already jeering him as he arrived at the finish. He did not stop to argue over his right to the winner's cheque. He legged it into the crowd and was not seen again. 'We couldn't catch him,' said joint race director Carine Verstraeten.

A Russian, Anatoly Karipanov, was the real winner, sporting a moustache apparently unchanged from start to finish.

THE PAINTED HORSE
Fine Cotton

The Fine Cotton racing scandal reads like a plot from *Only Fools and Horses*. It involved a decent horse being painted to look like a famous loser, with the crooks aiming to cash in when it won at long odds. But the plan was executed as shambolically as it might have been by Del Boy and Rodney – and the masterminds went to jail.

Fine Cotton was an Australian thoroughbred with a dismal track record. In a race between no-hopers, it would have been the rank outsider. But a betting syndicate had a bright idea – a scam which would cash in on the horse's notoriety throughout Queensland. They would buy a superior horse, closely resembling Fine Cotton, pass it off as the old nag and enter it in a race it was bound to win. The odds of Fine Cotton winning anything would be long indeed – so they would back it with as much money as they could and when the imposter won they would take the bookies to the cleaners.

Fine Cotton was entered for the Commerce Novice (Second Division) Handicap over 1,500 metres at Eagle Farm Racecourse, Brisbane, on 18 August 1984.

The plot was proceeding perfectly as race day approached. The villains had been able to buy a horse that was both fast and a dead ringer for Fine Cotton. No one would know the difference. But then the new horse went lame and could not race.

The syndicate had put too much time and money into the con to back out now. They set about finding a replacement, and secured a rather less than perfect one in a mount named Bold Personality. There was no problem with his form – the horse was a proven winner – but unfortunately it looked little like Fine Cotton. It was a seven-year-old bay gelding with no markings. Fine

Cotton, an eight-year-old brown gelding, had white markings on his hind legs.

The solution came in a flash – hair dye! The colourant was liberally applied all over the hapless beast to make it browner. It was only partly successful, but it would have to do.

The big day arrived, and the syndicate turned up to the track with their dyed horse. Suddenly, to their horror, they realised they had neglected to give Bold Personality any leg markings – a giveaway to anyone familiar with Fine Cotton. Worse, they had forgotten to bring along the peroxide they had originally intended to use for just this purpose.

Emergency measures were called for. Bold Personality's legs were sprayed with white paint. The result was a disaster – nothing like an animal's natural markings – so bandages were applied to conceal it.

The race was a Novice Handicap for up-and-coming young horses or older ones of little ability. Bold Personality, which was qualified for much higher calibre races, ought to win it with ease. However, in its disguise as Fine Cotton, its odds were 33-1.

The syndicate bet vast amounts on Fine Cotton to win, both at Eagle Farm and with bookies throughout Australia. If the scam paid off, they stood to pocket some £600,000 – worth many millions today.

By the time the race began, the deluge of money placed on Fine Cotton had seen its odds shorten to 7-2. But it had also already aroused the suspicion of the track stewards.

As predicted, Bold Personality was ridden to victory – by an unwitting apprentice unaware his mount was anything other than Fine Cotton. But stewards launched an immediate investigation into Fine Cotton's miraculous return to form and the huge amounts bet on him to win. By now, some minutes after the race, white paint was dribbling down Bold Personality's legs from beneath his bandages. Spectators noticed and some began to voice their concerns that the horse was an imposter.

Bookies were ordered to stop paying out on the result until Fine Cotton's trainer had been interviewed and the horse's registration papers examined. The papers could not be found. Neither could the trainer, who had run off.

Fine Cotton/Bold Personality was disqualified and the win given to the runner-up. The bookies were allowed to keep any money wagered on Fine Cotton, so the many punters who bet on him lost the lot. Police eventually traced the trainer in another part of Australia – and he and the scam's organiser were tried and jailed. Various other prominent Australian racing figures suspected of involvement were barred from the country's tracks.

As for Fine Cotton – the real Fine Cotton, that is – he retired from racing and lived to a ripe old age on the outskirts of Brisbane.

DIA, OH DIA, OH DIA
The Fake Footballer

Many a footballer has been sold a dummy. In Ali Dia, Southampton manager Graeme Souness was sold the biggest dummy in the Premiership's history. He was a player, signed under false pretences, whose spectacular ineptitude is still a source of hilarity for football fans more than a decade later.

Back in 1996, Souness was desperate to recruit another striker. When, out of the blue, he was phoned by FIFA's World Player of the Year, George Weah, recommending Dia, he thought Lady Luck had smiled on him.

Weah, an AC Milan superstar and a Liberian international, told the fiery Scot that Dia had played 13 times for Senegal and had a proven track record as a goal-scorer for club and country. Dia was available, Weah said, because he had just been released on a free transfer by Italian side Bologna. Weah added that Dia was his cousin – and that the two had played together at Paris St Germain.

Souness had never met Weah. But he had heard him speak on TV and radio and his voice seemed to match the one on the phone. As Souness said, 'When someone the calibre of George Weah calls to recommend a player, you tend to sit up and take notice.'

As it turned out, not one of the caller's claims was true... including his assertion that he was Weah. He was, in fact, Dia's agent, acting either on his own initiative or put up to it by Dia himself, depending on whose version of events you choose to believe.

Dia was, in reality, an amateur player at best, a reject from the lower leagues in France and Germany, with failed trials at Port Vale, Gillingham and Bournemouth behind him. Nonetheless, the hapless Souness signed Dia on a one-month contract and a magnificent footballing farce was in full swing.

Mother Nature threw in a contribution, washing out a reserve game against Arsenal that would have been Dia's first match for Southampton – and his last, had Souness been able to see him play.

Southampton's new arrival was talking a good game in the press. 'The Premiership is an exciting place to play,' said 31-year-old Dia. 'I feel I have a bit of pace and I can dribble well. Hopefully, I can now show enough of that to the manager and maybe get a place in his squad.'

He began training and took part in a five-a-side game. Team-mates noticed that he seemed like a fish out of water – but if George Weah had recommended him, how bad could he be? Besides, he was new to Britain and was probably still acclimatising. But the players were astonished when Souness, who had not seen Dia kick a ball, put him on the bench for a first-team Premiership clash with Leeds United on 23 November 1996.

After 32 minutes, Dia got his chance. Southampton's star striker, Matt Le Tissier, was injured and the man from Senegal ran on with all the confidence of a proven international. Within seconds, the truth began to dawn on everyone watching, Souness included. Dia, presented with an unmissable scoring opportunity from 12 yards, hoofed the ball straight to the goalkeeper.

He was obviously, horribly, out of his depth. The agony went on until half-time and for another eight minutes of the second half before Souness pulled the plug, substituting the substitute on 53 minutes.

The manager tried to put a brave face on the shambles. 'I don't feel I have been duped in the slightest,' he said. 'That's the way the world is these days. It cost us a couple of grand for two weeks' wages. It's not broken our hearts – and we certainly don't feel hard done by. He was an international player so we gave him a go, but he didn't impress and has now left the club. I have not met George Weah, but I have heard his voice on TV and radio and the man on the phone sounded similar.'

But Le Tissier knew his boss was smarting. 'Dia was worse than useless. It was the most bizarre situation I've ever come across,' he said years later. 'The day before the game he played in a five-a-side and looked like Bambi on ice, and we couldn't believe he was on the bench the next day. I don't know how he got there to this day and I'm sure Graeme Souness felt a bit stupid.

'I remember seeing Dia in the bath after the game. Then the next day he came in for treatment, saying he'd picked up an injury. We never saw him again.'

Dia was fired two weeks into his month's contract. He washed up at non-league Gateshead, before being transfer-listed there. He is most recently said to have studied for a degree at the University of Northumbria.

Dia always denied setting out to dupe Souness and blamed his agent. 'I never asked him to do it, but he was on 10 per cent of anything I earned. I've been made to look like a conman,' he protested.

Souness wasn't alone in falling for the patter of the bogus 'Weah' and his recommendation of Dia. Port Vale and Gillingham had already done so – but the former dumped the player after one reserve game and the latter did the same after a brief trial.

Gillingham boss Tony Pulis said, 'I was shocked to receive a call from someone claiming to be George Weah recommending a friend of his. I wouldn't have thought a man like Weah would have heard of Gillingham, but we gave the lad a trial.

'He was rubbish.'

LITTLE BIG MAN
Danny Almonte

Two weeks before 9/11, New York, and the rest of America, was engulfed by a shocking scandal – over the age of one Little League baseballer.

Danny Almonte was no ordinary player. The 12-year-old was a phenomenal pitcher with a devastating 77mph fastball that most adult players could not get near. The President, no less, was a fan.

Every parent in the United States knows the maximum age for Little League is 12. So the nationwide uproar when Almonte was outed as a 14-year-old was deafening. British readers will need to understand the scale of Little League and its importance to American life. Every community in the country has a Little League park, where kids while away the summer playing a reduced-size version of baseball as mom and dad watch from the stands. It is the embodiment of American wholesomeness – and millions take part.

The biggest event of the calendar is the Little League Baseball World Series, held every August in South Williamsport, Pennsylvania – the climax of the season's tournaments throughout the US and other countries. Its importance is such that President Bush, once a talented Little Leaguer himself, threw the opening ball of the world series in 2001.

Almonte, an immigrant from the Dominican Republic, led a mainly Hispanic team from the slums of New York's Bronx to third place in the World Series. In doing so, he threw the first 'perfect game' in 44 years – that is, he prevented any opposition batter from reaching first base, roughly equivalent to a bowler skittling an entire cricket team without conceding a run.

It was an incredible achievement. The All Stars, locally dubbed Las Bombardenitas del Bronx, received the keys of the city from New York Mayor Rudolph Giuliani.

Almonte signed autographs wherever he went and was the subject of a spread in the magazine *Newsweek*. He was a heart-throb to teenage girls who blew kisses to him as they hung around his team's compound during the World Series.

But several losing teams smelled a rat. They were sure Almonte's fastball was too good for any 12-year-old Little Leaguer. A group of parents involved with a rival New York outfit scraped $10,000 together to pay a private eye to probe Almonte's background.

Two days after the World Series, *Sports Illustrated* magazine turned up a birth certificate from his home country proving he was 14, not 12. Almonte's father Felipe had already produced one certificate 'proving' he was born on 7 April 1989, thus qualifying him for Little League. It was bogus. The earlier certificate recorded his delivery on 7 April 1987.

The president of Little League Inc was apoplectic. 'We have been deceived. A fraud has been perpetrated on Little League and millions of youngsters for whom Little League is so important,' said Stephen Keener.

President Bush weighed in, perhaps with a greater sense of perspective. 'I'm disappointed that adults would fudge the boy's age... but I wasn't disappointed in his fastball and his slider. The guy is awesome – he's a great pitcher.'

Almonte's mum Sonia insisted he was 12. 'I'm the mother,' she said. 'Who knows better than me?

People are jealous of what my son has done. If he hadn't been so successful, we wouldn't even be talking about this.'

Joan Dalmau, spokeswoman for the All Stars, added, 'It's all false. I feel it's a kind of discrimination. We are Latino. If we were white, this wouldn't have happened.'

The Bronx's Hispanic community was right behind Almonte, despite the blatant cheating. As the *New York Times* said, 'Almonte is viewed as a hero, and when he was born is mere nitpicking about statistics.'

In the end, there was no mercy. All the team's victories for the 2001 season were struck from the records, including Danny's 'perfect game'. Mayor Giuliani, soon to be a worldwide hero for his leadership after the World Trade Center attacks, displayed typical wisdom. He said he would not confiscate the keys to the city from the team. 'It would only add to the hurt and pain that the innocent children are already experiencing,' he said.

Almonte seemed unfazed by the scandal and went on to pitch successfully for one of America's top high school teams. Aged 19, he married a 30-year-old Manhattan hairdresser.

HERMAN THE GERMAN
Dora Ratjen

Such was Adolf Hitler's desperation for Aryan glory at his 1936 Berlin Olympics that he installed a bloke in his women's high-jump team.

The Führer was unlikely to let the trifling matter of 'Dora' Ratjen's true name or gender stand in his way. He had world domination in his sights, after all. In fact, if Dora's manly strength helped win gold for the Fatherland, all the better.

Dora took the place of a German Jew, Gretel Bergmann, sacked for allegedly mediocre performances even though she was a superb jumper who had equalled the European record.

Dora, a strapping lad with a husky voice, was instructed by his bosses in the Hitler Youth to bind up his genitals to avoid giving the game away. Nonetheless, his rivals – among them Surrey teenager Dorothy Odam – found his manly tones a giveaway. Dorothy said, 'I knew she was a man. You could tell by the voice and the build. But "she" was far from the only one. You could tell because they would always go into the toilet to get changed. We'd go and stand on the seat of the next-door cubicle or look under the door to see if we could catch them.'

In the end, the last laugh was on the Führer.

Dora came in fourth, behind three real women, including Britain's Dorothy.

In 1938, Dora was banned from further competitions due to his 'sexual ambiguity'. It was another 19 years – in 1957 – before he finally told all after being tracked down to a Bremen café where he was working as a waiter. He tearfully confessed that he was, in fact, Herman Ratjen – forced by the Nazis, he said, to pose as a woman 'for the sake of the honour and glory of Germany'. 'For three years I lived the life of a girl. It was most dull,' he said.

Herman – thereafter dubbed Herman the German – was not heard from again.

HE AIN'T HEAVY
The Motsoeneng Brothers

He lived in abject poverty with his parents and ten brothers and sisters in a South African shanty town, but Sergio Motsoeneng had one talent – long-distance running. And when the opportunity arose for a big payday to change all their lives, he decided to maximise his chances with the help of a younger brother who looked uncannily like him.

Sergio had run marathons before with considerable success. His personal best was a very respectable 2 hours 13 minutes. But that wasn't going to guarantee him a lucrative top-ten finish as the world's best runners met for South Africa's Comrades Ultra-Marathon in June 1999.

It was a gruelling 86km (56-mile) race from Pietermaritzburg to Durban, the most demanding athletics event in the southern hemisphere, and that year attracted an international field of 20,000, competing to share a 610,000 rand prize (then worth £61,000).

Sergio, 21, was driven to the event by Dewalt Steyn, manager of his athletics team, for the 6am start. Each of the runners, among them British legend Steve Cram, had a microchip embedded in their left shoe to record their exact time from start to finish.

Sergio's subterfuge began after 20km. Looking around to check there were no familiar faces in the crowd, he popped into one of the portable toilets along the route and nipped inside a cubicle. A few minutes later, he emerged to rejoin the race, and no one was any the wiser.

Except Sergio had not emerged. Instead, it was his brother Sefako, 19, with whom Sergio had swapped clothes – microchipped trainers included.

Sefako was also a talented runner and, importantly, a fresh pair of legs to run the second 20km. He set off, and Sergio waited until the coast was clear before emerging, in Sefako's clothes, to catch a cab to the race's half-way point. There, he entered another toilet and, after a few minutes, was joined by Sefako for a second swap. The plan almost went wrong at that moment. Sergio's team manager Steyn turned up and waited outside the toilet to give Sergio an energy drink.

Sergio said later, 'We held our breath before changing very slowly and, after ten minutes, Dewalt left.' Sergio rejoined the race and Sefako caught a taxi home to watch the rest on TV.

Guilt and fear consumed Sergio as he ran. 'I wanted to move up the positions but doubt came into my mind as I realised somebody may have seen us. At around 70km, Dewalt told me to push on – that's when I realised he did not know what had happened. I crossed the finish line ninth and my heart was beating fast, because I remember from my parents that when you do something wrong, you can't hide. Dewalt came to me and said, "Sergio, you finished in the top ten, why can't you be happy?"'

Sergio was gaining confidence and starting to assume he had got away with it. But he hadn't counted on the tenacity of a rival, Nick Bester, who finished 13th and was determined to prove Sergio hadn't got the better of him.

It took a month or two, but Bester trawled through hundreds of pictures taken by the official race photographers before finding two that confirmed his suspicions. Both seemed to show Sergio running the race of his life. But in one he had a pink watch on his right wrist. In the other, he wore a yellow watch on his left.

Bester was ready to tell the world the story. But a local lawyer, Clem Harrington, who knew the Motsoenengs and had himself run the same race 21 times, stepped in. 'I was faxed the pictures and could tell that they were different people. I told the brothers they would never get away with it,' he said. Harrington convinced the sneaky pair to confess to officials and return their winner's medal. But their cash prize – 6,000 rand, or £600, a fortune for poor South Africans – was another matter. The boys insisted they had given it to their father, but the money was nowhere to be found when organisers of the charity race demanded it back.

'I suspect the brothers spent it on themselves,' Harrington said. 'In the end, we sold the story to a magazine in order to repay Comrades. Sergio lives with his parents and ten brothers and sisters in a two-bedroomed house, and the family had run into financial difficulties. That's why the brothers tried to pull off the trick.'

Sergio was hit with a three-year ban from all athletics in South Africa and a ten-year ban from the Comrades event.

'If I could run the race again, I would never do what I did,' he said. 'The bans mean my time as a runner has passed. I'm sorry about what I did. If we weren't so poor, we would not have done it. We'd have made sure there was enough food for everyone. I wanted that money so badly.'

THE WOMAN WHO WASN'T
Indian Runner Santhi Soundarajan

A silver medallist in a prestigious 800-metre race for women was disqualified and stripped of her gong – after she turned out to be a man.

Santhi Soundarajan, said to be India's best athlete, came second at the 2006 Asian Games in Doha, Qatar. It was just one in a string of triumphs. She had previously set the national record in the 3,000 metres steeplechase, and in one event in Bangalore won all three middle-distance events – the 800, 1,500 and 3,000 metres.

After her silver in the Asian Games, she failed a routine sex test carried out by a team of medics including a gynaecologist and a psychologist. Their report to the Indian Olympic Association said she 'does not possess the sexual characteristics of a woman'.

Lalit Bhanot, of the Athletics Federation of

India, said Soundarajan failed on 'a technicality' but did not elaborate. It was not known whether the technicality was the presence of a male organ.

Soundarajan, then 25, was listed as a girl on her birth certificate, went to a girls' school and had apparently passed previous sex tests. Her coach P Nagarajan said she was raised in extreme poverty and barely ate any decent meals until she was 23. Malnourishment, he explained, can cause severe hormone imbalances. He called the test result 'very sad and extremely disappointing'.

Friends of the athlete said she would never have taken male hormones to improve her performance and that the problem was naturally occurring. Soundarajan, distraught, said, 'My conscience is very clear. I have done nothing wrong.'

NAGGING SUSPICION
Flockton Grey

When a virtually unknown two-year-old racehorse named Flockton Grey stormed to victory over a short course by an astonishing 20 lengths, there were two possibilities – it was destined to become an all-time great, or it was not Flockton Grey.

British racing's greatest 'ringer' scandal came on

29 March 1982, when Flockton, an unfancied gelding, made its track debut at Leicester in a race for two-year-olds. Its odds were 10-1 and, at that price, it was heavily backed – mainly by its dodgy owner Ken Richardson. He was a businessman and gambler, a self-made millionaire twice over, with a bankruptcy between his fortunes. Richardson had £20,000 on his horse, placed with several bookies, and stood to win £200,000, a gigantic sum in 1982.

Flockton easily won the race – held over just five furlongs, or about one kilometre – and was then whisked away from the track before the stewards could hold an inquiry. The winning horse was, of course, a lookalike – an experienced three-year-old called Good Hand, also owned by Richardson.

The winning margin was so suspicious that the bookies refused to pay up. Police were called in. Since the horse had vanished without trace, the only evidence was from a photographer who had managed to snap it with its mouth open. Vets said its teeth were those of a three-year-old, not a two-year-old. It also had a distinctive scar on one leg. Investigators finally traced the real Flockton Grey to a yard run by trainer Stephen Wiles – and found no such scar.

In court, 46-year-old Richardson, defended by the great QC George Carman, insisted the winning horse was Flockton Grey. It was no use. He was handed a nine-month suspended jail term and a £20,000 fine. He was also banned from racing for 25 years – a severe punishment for a big-time gambler.

Good Hand's jockey Kevin Darley was exonerated. He had no idea his mount wasn't Flockton Grey – and it was pointed out that, had he known, he could easily have held the horse back to make the winning margin less suspicious.

Richardson never gave up the battle to prove his innocence. Over the next eleven years, he lost two appeals. A third appeal seemed to have a greater chance when new evidence cast doubt on whether Good Hand was the winning horse. But Richardson lost that, too.

His life then took a disastrous turn in 1999 when, as owner of Doncaster Rovers Football Club, he was convicted of a plot to burn down their ground's main stand for the insurance money. Aged 61 by then, he was jailed for four years.

Chapter 6

Fiddlers

TAMPER, TAMPER
Imran Khan and Waqar Younis

One afternoon on the cricket ground at Hove in
1981, Hampshire were 105 for 2, grinding out a
draw against Sussex. The Sussex bowlers simply
could not make the breakthrough. Then their great
all-rounder Imran Khan did something that would
reverberate 25 years later: He ordered a bottle top
to be sent out from the pavilion and secretly
gouged the ball with it. Hampshire's last eight
wickets tumbled in quick succession and they lost
by nine wickets.

It was an infamous act of cheating. By the time

Imran finally admitted to it in 1994, controversy was already raging about ball-tampering by Pakistan's cricketers. He threw petrol on the flames.

Artificially altering a ball's condition aids a bowler by exaggerating its movement through the air or causing it to move in a way the batsman does not expect. Of course, it would be ludicrous to suggest that Pakistan has a monopoly on the illegal practice. It is probably as old as the game itself. But it only became an emotive issue with the invention by Pakistani bowlers of the devastating technique of 'reverse swing'. This involves the ball, bowled very fast, swinging late in its flight in exactly the opposite direction to that which the batsman expects. It is only possible when one side of the ball is much rougher than the other, which can be achieved either through normal wear and tear or by deliberately, illegally, scuffing up the ball.

The Pakistani bowler Sarfraz Nawaz developed reverse swing in the 1970s and passed it on to Imran. He used it to become one of the finest all-rounders in the history of the game, taking 362 Test match wickets and, aged 39, captaining Pakistan to World Cup glory in 1992.

The bottle-top confession was buried away in an authorised biography. 'Scratching the ball or lifting the seam has gone on ever since cricket has been played and, within limits, this was accepted as part of the game,' Imran said. 'I occasionally scratched the side of the ball and lifted the seam.

'When Sussex were playing Hampshire in 1981 and the ball was not deviating at all, I got our 12th man to bring a bottle top out and the ball started to move around a lot.' He added, 'I was surprised at the naïveté of journalists who seem to have discovered this new form of cheating only two years back.' This last remark referred to Pakistan's explosive 1992 tour of England, which triggered a huge cheating storm.

Pakistan's fearsome fast-bowling pair of Wasim Akram and Waqar Younis repeatedly destroyed England with reverse swing and won the Test series 2-1. But mutterings about ball-tampering went on all through a bad-tempered summer. Eventually, during the lunch interval of a one-day international at Lord's, the umpires changed the match ball because it was damaged. No reason was given publicly. But England batsman Allan Lamb then caused a furore by admitting he had tipped off the umpires to the Pakistanis' behaviour, and that all summer they had been gouging the ball with their fingernails. He told the *Daily Mirror*, 'I blew the whistle on Pakistan's ball-tampering tricks. They have repeatedly tampered with the ball to produce murderous late swing. I just couldn't stand by and see them getting away with breaking the laws of cricket time and again. When I went out to bat at Lord's and saw them up to their old tricks, I alerted the umpires.

'I pointed to a few scuff marks on the ball and told the umpires, "Keep your eyes on those and you'll see them get bigger." Sure enough, by lunch, the scuffmarks had grown alarmingly. The umpires took the ball to the match referee at lunch and, when I came out to resume my innings, they told me, "The ball has been changed."

Lamb claimed Sarfraz, with whom he played, invented the practice and passed it on to Pakistani team-mates (Sarfraz later sued for libel, but withdrew the case when Lamb conceded that he never cheated in games they played together).

Cricket authorities fined Lamb £5,000 for speaking out and he never played for England again.

Waqar and Wasim were incensed, saying in a joint statement, 'We categorically deny that we have ever cheated or tampered illegally with any match ball in any game during our careers. The allegations made are deeply offensive to us and the entire Pakistani team. It is significant that these allegations are only now being made after we have beaten England in a Test series. When we have been on the losing side in county or Test cricket, nothing has been said.'

They had their supporters, too, even in the England camp. John Lever, the former England and Essex swing bowler, said the damage to the ball was due solely to wear and tear. 'The fact is Wasim and Waqar are two of the best Test bowlers we've seen in this country for a long time and we won't see another pair like them for 20 years,' he said.

The row rumbled on for two years with Pakistan still protesting their innocence. The difficulty for umpires was actually catching a player in the act. Six years later, in 2000, Waqar was caught. He became the first player in cricket history suspended for ball-tampering when TV cameras showed him gouging the ball in a match against South Africa. The great Indian batsman Sachin Tendulkar became the second, being handed a one-match ban in 2001 for scratching the ball with his fingers while bowling. Pakistan's fast bowler Shoaib Akhtar then fell foul of the rules in both 2002 and 2003.

In 2006, the issue brought about one of cricket's biggest ever crises. At the Oval, in the fourth Test of a series between England and Pakistan, Australian umpire Darrell Hair suddenly inspected the ball and decided it had been tampered with by the Pakistanis. He awarded five penalty runs against them and ordered the ball to be changed.

After the tea interval, Pakistan's captain Inzamam-ul-Haq and his players remained in the pavilion in protest, saying Hair had no proof that the ball had been interfered with. The umpires waited on the pitch for several minutes, then went to the Pakistan dressing room to ask if they intended to play on. They did not get a reply. The umpires returned to the wicket, removed the bails and awarded the match to England – the first forfeited game in the history of Test cricket. By the time the Pakistanis were ready to play on, they emerged on to the field to find the match over.

There was never any proof they had cheated – and, as a result, the umpire received more criticism than the players. At a disciplinary hearing, Inzamam was cleared of ball-tampering but was banned for four one-day internationals for bringing the game into disrepute over the sit-in.

The resulting analysis of the Oval fiasco by cricket experts from both England and Pakistan produced an amazing confession about the infamous earlier tour in 1992.

Rameez Raja, the former Pakistan batsman, admitted that, despite repeated denials, the ball had been tampered with. Raja said, 'At certain moments, the ball was tampered with. At times, it wasn't and still the ball was made to reverse-swing by the quality of Waqar and Wasim's bowling. The whole point was to enlarge the scuffed-up area. Ball-tampering doesn't guarantee you success. It's not such a diabolical issue as far as I'm concerned.'

Another, more revealing confession came in a book by the veteran Pakistani spin bowler Mushtaq Ahmed, who made his international debut in 1989. 'When I started playing for Pakistan,' he said, 'it was quite normal for the ball to be scratched and tampered with during a match. The batsmen and umpires in the 1980s and 1990s had no idea... some players were experts at doing it.'

FOILED AGAIN
Boris Onischenko

It had the makings of a Bond movie – a KGB colonel using a secret electronic device to 'kill off' his arch-rival from the British Army at the height of the Cold War, causing an international incident. OK, it was only the fencing competition in the Modern Pentathlon event at the 1976 Montréal Olympics, but it was one of the most cunning acts of cheating in the annals of sport. The Soviets' golden boy rigged his sword to trigger the electronic scoreboard even if it didn't hit his opponent.

It is a wonder why Boris Onischenko felt the need to cheat in the first place. He was a terrific all-round athlete who had won Olympic silver four years earlier and finished in the top three in every world championship from 1969 to 1974. He was unquestionably the best fencer in his event.

After the first of the pentathlon's five disciplines, horse-riding, Britain's three-man team, captained by army sergeant Jim Fox, was lying in the bronze medal position. But their 76-point lead over the Soviets was uncomfortably slim. They knew the Russians were likely to leapfrog them after the fencing, at which they reigned supreme.

To understand what happened next it is important to know how scoring works in electric epée fencing. The epée (sword) is wired to a scoring box. Each fencer also has wires beneath his jacket. When one fencer's epee touches the opponent, it completes a circuit and registers as a hit.

Onischenko fitted the handle of his epée with a tiny button which allowed him to make the circuit without hitting the opponent. He could register a hit at will – though, to be convincing, it was obviously crucial to trigger it only when he thrust the sword close to his rival.

First to face Onischenko was Britain's specialist swimmer, Adrian Parker. He was expected to lose to such a superior fencer, of course – but Fox, standing on the sidelines, was troubled by what he saw. He became convinced that the scoring box was registering hits for the Soviet without contact being made.

He put his hunch to the test the moment he faced Onischenko himself. At the Soviet's first thrust, Fox swayed back so far that the tip of the sword was six inches from him – yet still the scoring light came on. Fox complained, and the officials took Onischenko's sword away for tests for a possible short-circuit. Not that replacing the suspect sword made much difference to the Soviet's impressive form – he beat Fox, and won eight of his nine bouts that day.

Fox, however, knew something was wrong from a remark the Soviet made to him as they passed each other in the stadium. They knew each other well – they had drunk together at previous tournaments. Onischenko suddenly said, 'Jim, I am very sorry.'

The motive behind the cryptic apology became clear when the technicians reported what they had found in the Soviet's sword – not a short-circuit, but a push-button circuit-breaker built into the handle.

The press loved the story. Onischenko was dubbed 'Boris the Cheat' and – by one particularly inspired sub-editor – 'Disonischenko'. Onischenko and his pentathlon team were disqualified, to the outrage of the Soviet Union.

From that point, the crisis escalated. This was the Cold War. Onischenko was a half-colonel in the KGB and Fox a sergeant in the British Army. The significance could not have been greater. There were rumours that Eastern Bloc nations would abandon the Games en masse. But it was eventually accepted that Onischenko had been caught bang to rights. Before reporters could get to him, he was bundled out of Canada and back to the Ukraine, his glittering athletics career at an abrupt and ignominious end.

Fox felt for Onischenko, a man he had known and competed against for ten years, and the stress of the scandal wrecked his performances. 'Boris and I weren't bosom pals,' he said later. 'But we'd often drunk vodka together in the evenings at various competitions, so there was a relationship between us. They sent him down the docks and home. Can you imagine it? Because it was only the second day of the Olympics and there were no finals on, the press just rushed in from all over the place. They interrupted our competition to hold a press conference, so I fenced like a dog.

'It became a huge international incident. At one stage, I was told the whole Eastern Bloc was going to pull out, and it was down to me. It's not ideal material for a competitor to be thinking about, is it?'

Demoralised, Fox shot his pistol the following day worse than he had fenced. Britain slumped to eighth place. But on the fourth day, Parker swam brilliantly to drag them back to fifth. On the last day, Fox, already 36, ran superbly in the cross-country to snatch gold for the team.

Thirty years on from Montréal, Fox still felt sad for Onischenko. 'The Soviets stripped him of all his titles,' he said. 'He's a taxi driver now.'

CORKING EXCUSE
Sammy Sosa

Sammy Sosa was a baseball legend, fifth in the all-time list of home-run scorers. But a question mark hangs over his tally... after he was found to be using a dodgy bat.

'Corking' a baseball bat is a well-known scam. It involves drilling a core of wood about six inches long out of the heavy end and filling the hole with cork or sawdust, before sealing it back up. The result is a lighter bat, which speeds up the batter's swing and probably improves his timing, without making a huge difference to its impact on the ball. Corked bats are banned.

Sosa, nicknamed 'Slammin' Sammy', was one of America's most popular sportsmen and a star with the Chicago Cubs. But he fell from grace during a match against Tampa Bay in June 2003 when his bat split as it hit the ball. Umpire Tim McClelland, who picked it up, said, 'I turned it over and there was a half-dollar-sized piece of cork in the bat, half-way up the barrel.'

Sosa was barred from the match and his other bats – all 76 of them – confiscated. Tests showed they were all legitimate.

Sosa, an exuberant 34-year-old from the Dominican Republic, said the corked bat was meant for practice only – and that he took it on to the field by accident. His many fans felt betrayed. One writer in the *Chicago Tribune* said, 'It's as if someone had caught Superman using brass knuckles, or suspected Robin Hood of stealing from the poor, or accused King Arthur of rigging it so that the sword would slide easily out of the stone.'

Sosa was barred from baseball for seven games, then went through three fallow seasons before making a comeback in 2007 with the Texas Rangers.

Joe Torre, long-time manager of the New York Yankees, said of Sosa's corked bat, 'Unfortunately, it's a dirty mark, when you consider all he's accomplished.'

A BAT OUT OF HELL
Dennis Lillee

One of the great fast bowlers of cricket history, Dennis Lillee was a destroyer of many a batting line-up. In 1979, he was very nearly the destroyer of a ball, after taking the crease against England with a bat made from aluminium.

Lillee, batting for Australia at the start of the second day of a Test match in Perth, shunned the traditional willow for a metal bat made by a firm he was involved with and keen to promote.

England's fielders took little notice at first. But their ears pricked up when Lillee hit his first ball and the customary, satisfying knock of leather-on-willow was replaced by the harsh clunk of leather-on-metal. Fielders inspected the ball, and found a gouge. The same thing happened with the next ball and England's captain Mike Brearley complained to the umpires.

A ten-minute row ensued during which Lillee rightly pointed out that he was not cheating. The laws of cricket did not specify that bats must be wooden. Brearley accepted this, but said there were also rules about knowingly damaging the ball. Sanity prevailed when Lillee's captain Greg Chappell ordered him to change his bat. He did so, after defiantly launching the aluminium version 40 yards in the direction of the pavilion.

The rules were quickly changed to stipulate bats must be wooden. Lillee, according to one account, was left with a garage full of unsold aluminium bats.

Chapter 7

Tricksters

THE DUBIOUS HAT
Indian Chess Schemer

When a virtual chess unknown rocketed from obscurity up the world rankings, officials smelled a rat. A quick check revealed that he was receiving outside help via a listening device in his hat.

Umakanth Sharma, 25, was a chess journeyman, ranked outside the world's top 50,000 during 2005. But within nine months, his rating leapt beyond that of an International Master, placing him a much more respectable 1,643rd. The speed of his improvement was unprecedented in the annals of the 1,500-year-old game. Furthermore, when one 'victim' fed his game against Sharma into a computer program, he found it made exactly the moves Sharma made.

Sharma was finally busted at a prestigious tournament at an Indian air force base in Delhi. A routine frisking by an air force official with a metal detector uncovered a Bluetooth device stitched into the lining of his cap, which he liked to pull down over his ears at all times, especially during games. The gizmo allowed him to hear whispered instructions from friends outside the tournament who were feeding the moves of each game he played into their computer and relaying the machine's suggested move back to him.

Chess bosses looked into Sharma's background and even his finances. 'We were surprised to learn that he had an expensive mobile phone despite being unemployed,' said a spokesman. 'It is only recently that he got a job with the railways.'

Sharma was kicked out of the tournament and banned from chess for ten years. But it was still a mystery how he was able to convey each move to his accomplices without drawing attention.

NO WINNINGS, NO CRY
A Rastafarian Rogue

Few attempts to cheat at chess can have been more blatant than that of a Rastafarian who tried to win prize money in the 'unrated players' section at the World Open in Philadelphia in 1993.

The unknown contestant had a sense of irony, though, signing in as John von Neumann, in reality the name of a pioneer of computing and artificial intelligence. He fared impressively in the Open section, scoring 4.5 points out of a possible 9, in the process drawing a match with a Grandmaster and beating a player with a rating around that of an International Master. However, his long dreadlocks only partially concealed the headphones he wore throughout each game and refused to remove. One pocket bulged with a device he repeatedly pressed as the game progressed and which he presumably hoped people would take for a Walkman.

Eventually, he was challenged by the tournament organiser – and, on questioning, proved clueless about even the most basic chess tactics. It is suspected he was relaying his opponents' moves to a friend parked outside the venue, and receiving recommended moves back, probably generated by a computer program.

FAKER IN THE FOG
Jockey Sylvester Carmouche

Some acts of sporting skulduggery are shrouded in mystery. In the case of cheating jockey Sylvester Carmouche, his horse was shrouded in mist.

Carmouche was riding a 23-1 outsider called Landing Officer at the Delta Downs Racetrack in Louisiana on the afternoon of 11 January 1990 when a pea-souper of a fog descended, reducing visibility to a matter of inches. Punters couldn't see a thing. But suddenly they were aware of Landing Officer galloping over the finish line of the mile-long race an amazing 24 lengths clear. Despite the appalling conditions, the horse was within 1.2 seconds of the track record.

Racing chiefs were suspicious, especially as course monitors reported counting eight horses crossing the line after the first lap and nine after the second. Even more odd was that Landing Officer had barely broken a sweat and was breathing remarkably regularly for a horse that came within a whisker of the track record.

The truth was that crafty Carmouche had stopped his mount in the fog almost as soon as he left the starting gate, allowing the rest of the field to gallop by, before wandering over to the back straight and waiting for the sound of pounding

The king of cheats Ben Johnson storms to victory in the dirtiest Olympic 100 metres final in history.

Above: Hitting the bottle – Olympic champion swimmer Michelle Smith's urine sample contained a huge amount of whisky, which earned her a four-year ban.   © *News Group Newspapers*

Below: Roy Jones looks on in amazement as he is robbed of gold at the 1988 Seoul Olympics.

Kristin Otto: six Olympic golds and 'more testosterone in her than the
entire starting team of the Dallas Cowboys.'

© AP

Above: Even by the standards of most referees, Robert Hoyzer is a real hate figure in Germany – he was involved in match-fixing in 2005.

© *Getty*

Below: Ali Dia, 'cousin of George Weah' and Graeme Souness's most famous signing for Southampton. Souness didn't make the same mistake during his tenure as Newcastle boss, however – the Magpies kit Dia is wearing here is for a Geordie amateur side. © *News Group Newspapers*

Above: Rosie Ruiz, the marathon winner who only ran half a mile.

© *Corbis*

Below: Ffyona Campbell, on her abridged journey around the world.

© *PA*

Donald Crowhurst (above) and his boat, the *Teignmouth Electron* (left).

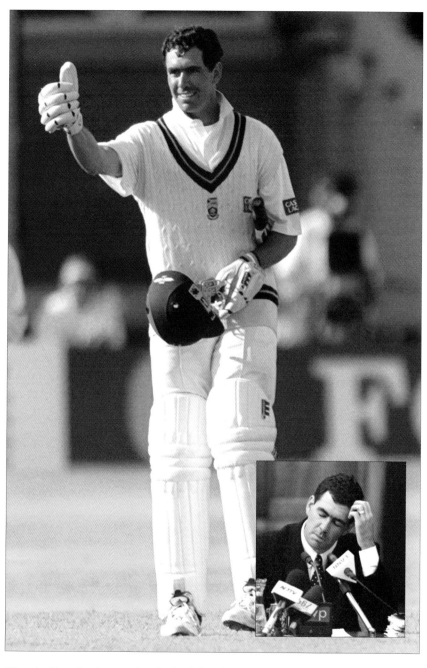

Hansie Cronje, the much-admired South African cricket captain, and his spectacular fall from grace (inset).

The Turk: the machine that fooled the world for 80 years.

hooves as they came round again. Hidden by the mist, he rejoined the race at full tilt, and well ahead of the pack, for the dash to the line – his fresh horse leaving its exhausted rivals trailing in its wake.

Unfortunately, Carmouche miscalculated. So overwhelming was his victory that it was bound to come under scrutiny. Had he waited a while longer and won by a nose he might have got away with it.

Carmouche, 28, mounted a forceful and succinct defence before the Louisiana State Racing Commission. 'I ain't did it,' he told them. But other jockeys swore he never overtook them at any stage – and Carmouche's fate was sealed. Racing chiefs voted by 7-1 to ban him. The sole dissenting voice was either convinced by his denial, or believed that hiding a horse in the fog and rejoining a race for the last few hundred yards was insufficiently underhand to warrant a ban.

Carmouche was suspended from racing in the state for ten years for 'failure to race the entire course'. He maintained his denials until an appeal in 1993, when he finally came clean. But he was made to serve eight years of his ban before he got his licence back in 1998.

Carmouche resumed his career as a successful jockey. And his transgression didn't dissuade his two sons from following in his footsteps, although they are often asked if they are the 'fog jockey'.

'I guess we will never hear the end of it,' says Carmouche's son Kendrick.

WATER MITTY
The Sad Tale of Donald Crowhurst

Few cheats deserve our sympathy. Donald Crowhurst – who fooled millions as he pretended to sail round the world – undoubtedly does.

Crowhurst's deception was on a grand scale. A failing businessman, he entered a lucrative competition set up by the *Sunday Times* in 1968 to find the first person able to sail single-handed, non-stop around the world. It was prompted by Sir Francis Chichester's successful voyage a year earlier, which had entailed a stop in Sydney.

To say the least, Crowhurst was an unlikely entrant. His race rivals were all established sea dogs; he was, at best, a weekend sailor. But the 36-year-old married father-of-four was desperate to be fêted as a hero. He also needed the £5,000 prize money to bail out his failing business, making marine and aviation navigation systems, and put his often-broke family on a secure financial footing.

His chances were nil, his preparations woefully inadequate. The boat he had built, the *Teignmouth*

Electron, was a 40ft trimaran untested on such a long voyage. Nonetheless, he secured sponsors, chief among them Stanley Best, a West Country caravans tycoon who made Crowhurst agree to pay back every penny if the voyage was abandoned.

Another associate, Rodney Hallworth, a former Fleet Street reporter, whipped up publicity based on the plucky underdog challenging the giants of sailing.

The 27,000-mile route involved sailing south from Britain through the Atlantic, around the Cape of Good Hope at the southern tip of Africa, east across the Indian and Pacific Oceans, past Australia and New Zealand, around Cape Horn at the southern tip of South America, and northwards back to Britain.

Crowhurst finally set sail from Devon to live out his mad fantasy. In the panic to set off before the deadline – he left on the last day allowed under the rules – he left vital supplies and spares behind. Problems began almost immediately and the wannabe hero was making only half the speed he had planned.

As he meandered slowly south through the Atlantic, Crowhurst was hopelessly behind his rivals and his boat was leaking. This was manageable in calm seas, where he could bail out water by hand. But if he ever made it to the storm-lashed Southern Ocean, he would sink like a stone.

What was he to do? His entire life – his family, his business, his self-esteem – hinged on a crazy venture he had foolishly undertaken. If he admitted defeat and turned back, he would be a national joke. Worse still, his main sponsor would demand the agreed refund and bankrupt him.

To plough on, though, spelled certain disaster, not to mention death. Cheating seemed like the only way out. In 1969, there were no global positioning systems or satellite navigation. Only by radio could he betray his position. So Crowhurst figured that if he communicated with his back-up team in England by telegram, and maintained radio silence for long periods, no one would know that he was anywhere other than where he falsely claimed to be.

The Walter Mitty of world sailing reported that he was making terrific progress and was chasing the pack hard. His team passed on the news to the press and suddenly, up and down Britain, Crowhurst had the celebrity he craved – the novice underdog challenging sailing's élite for the ultimate accolade.

In reality, he was sailing round and round in a huge circle off South America. His plan was to wait until his rivals came back that way on the return leg and then, 100 miles out of their sight, rejoin them and dash for the finish. Crowhurst knew that if he won the race outright his logbooks would never stand up to the scrutiny which experienced sailors would inevitably subject them to. More than anything, their entries betrayed a writer whose mental state was falling apart. He knew he would be exposed as a conman.

The safest option, he thought, was to play the 'valiant runner-up', coming in second or third against overwhelming odds... and dodging the full glare of the spotlight. But two pieces of bad luck scuppered his plan. First, the French sailor Bernard Moitessier, who stood a good chance of winning, decided not to finish the race by returning to England and sailed instead to Polynesia.

Then Nigel Tetley, a Royal Navy commander sailing a trimaran, sank less than 1,100 miles from home. His vessel had been falling apart, but instead of limping to the finish he sailed it as hard as he could, because he was told Crowhurst was on his tail. Tetley was rescued and later given £1,000 compensation by the organisers.

That left Robin Knox-Johnston to win the race, but he had set off months before Crowhurst, who was bound to finish in the fastest time and bag the top prize.

Back home, Britain was rooting for the underdog, as expected. Hallworth, Crowhurst's publicity man, told him 100,000 people would be flocking to Teignmouth to wave him in. He would be the nation's darling.

It was too much. Crowhurst was tormented by his huge deception of the people of Britain and could not face the humiliation of being exposed. His last diary entry, on 1 July 1969, reads, 'It is finished, it is finished. It is the mercy. It is the end of my game.'

Crowhurst's body was never found. Whether he jumped to his death, or fell overboard in a state of confusion, will never be known. On board his yacht, found on 10 July 1969, were taped confessions, as well as his anguished log entries.

Knox-Johnston thus became the first man to sail single-handed, non-stop round the world. He gave his £5,000 prize to Crowhurst's widow.

EARS WHAT WE'LL DO
Hansie Cronje and Bob Woolmer

A year before he was exposed as a match-fixer, Hansie Cronje was involved in another 'cheating' controversy – but this time the architect was his coach, ex-England star Bob Woolmer.

The South African captain and his opening bowler Allan Donald took to the field during a

World Cup match against India wearing earpieces allowing them to receive instructions from Woolmer, watching the match from the dressing room.

Woolmer, a fearless and unconventional coach, saw nothing wrong with his hi-tech ruse. After all, he reasoned, coaches regularly issued instructions via a Twelfth Man sent on to the field on the pretext of delivering new gloves or a drink. The earpieces, he said, merely speeded things up.

Indeed, there was nothing in the rules to prevent such a ploy, so technically it was not cheating. But it was hardly in the spirit of fair play.

Cronje and Donald only had the benefit of Woolmer's wisdom for about an hour before the referee at the match in Hove, Sussex, ordered them to remove their earpieces.

The International Cricket Council made its displeasure known. It said, 'The World Cup is not the event to experiment with new devices without first seeking permission from the ICC.'

Woolmer said, 'If I have upset anyone, I apologise. I was just trying to be innovative. We probably should have asked permission from the ICC. I suppose it was a little naïve of me not to do that.'

South Africa's cricket chief Ali Bacher admitted he had frowned on the idea when Woolmer first suggested it. 'Games are won by astute captains and we would not want experts dictating to the captain, the batsman or the bowler what he should be doing on the field,' he said. 'Bob came to me to ask about it and I told him it could be controversial. But Bob has a hyperactive cricket brain and sometimes he gets ahead of himself.'

Even without their radio link, South Africa won the match.

THE BOGUS RACE MEETING
Mr Martin's Great Sting

The greatest sting in British sporting history beggars belief in its scope and audacity. A criminal gang invented an entire day's racing – the horses, the riders, even the course – and suckered bookies into paying out a fortune on the results. The crooks made off with an amount worth millions today and were never caught.

In late July of 1898, a top-hatted gent calling himself Mr G Martin and hailing from St Ives, Cornwall, turned up at the offices of *The Sportsman*, a daily sports newspaper in London. He offered to provide the paper with details of all the races being held at Trodmore in Cornwall on 1 August. It was a Bank Holiday, a busy day for racegoers and racing journalists, so the paper was keen to get any help it could. It agreed to print the race card and accepted Mr Martin's offer that, for a small fee, he would send over the results on the day by telegram.

No one questioned Mr Martin's credentials, nor the existence of Trodmore, nor the names of any of the horses or riders. *The Sportsman* printed the card on the day of the race and the gang got to work. Clutching copies of the paper, they toured London's street bookies, pointing out the relevant page and betting heavily on favourites. The odds were never better than 5-1 – attractive, but not long enough to raise suspicions. One horse, at 5-1 in the fourth race, was 'Reaper'.

In the late afternoon, Mr Martin wired over the results, which appeared in the next day's *Sportsman*. That was good enough for some bookies, who paid out huge sums to the gang. Others held back the winnings, baffled that the results had not also appeared in a rival racing paper, the *Sporting Life*. So Mr Martin arranged for the *Sporting Life* to publish them, too.

An unfortunate typesetting error there cost the gang an even greater fortune. The paper gave Reaper's odds as 5-2 instead of the 5-1 printed in *The Sportsman*. The bookies began asking questions. 'Which odds were correct?' 'How come we've never heard of Reaper?' 'Or Trodmore?'

None of them existed. And soon it was as if Mr Martin and his gang had never existed either. They vanished without trace with as much as £100,000 in ill-gotten gains.

KING-SIZED HOAX
The 'Turk' Chess Machine

A loose definition of cheating allows us to detail one of the great hoaxes of history – a chess-playing clockwork mannequin known as 'The Turk', whose secret was so well kept that it fooled the world for 80 years.

It was a mechanical contraption of fantastic complexity, designed, built and unveiled by a Hungarian baron, Wolfgang von Kempelen, in 1770. The Turk comprised the upper half of a man, made from wood and dressed like an Arab sorcerer, seated behind a large cabinet, on top of which was a chess board. Inside the cabinet, available for anyone to view, was an intricate set of clockwork pulleys, cogs and wires, and seemingly nothing else. When wound up, the Turk – then known as the Great Chess Automaton – played with enormous skill, moving the magnetic pieces himself and even saying 'Check' at the appropriate moment. The Turk toured the world for decades, conquering many strong chess players. Plenty were sure it was for real. Even sceptics had no idea how it was done. Only those inside the owner's close circle of accomplices knew the Turk's secret – it was operated by a champion chess player hiding in the cabinet.

As a magic trick, The Turk was a masterpiece that stood up to the closest examination. Before every show, Kempelen opened the cabinet's sliding doors to prove that only clockwork-style machinery lay within. If he opened the rear doors, too, viewers could see right through the cabinet. But it was an illusion. Kempelen had allowed space for a man to hide in the cabinet even as it was being inspected. The operator sat on a rolling chair linked to a series of sliding panels. As Kempelen opened more doors, his accomplice rolled to another hiding place – the chair's movement automatically closing and opening new panels and bringing into view dummy machinery.

Kempelen was able to get some of Europe's finest chess players to operate his machine. Once play was under way, they would register their opponent's moves above their head by the movements of magnets on the underside of the board. The 'operator' would replicate these on his own miniature board within the cabinet. A further piece of mechanical brilliance allowed the Turk to grasp and move its pieces. It involved a series of levers that linked the operator's tiny board with the Turk's left arm. The operator moved a metal pointer to his desired square – and the Turk would shift its hand to the same square on its board. Turning the lever opened and closed the Turk's hand.

Kempelen toured Europe with the Turk. Later, a new owner took it to America. In the hands of skilled operators – among them the English chess champion William Lewis – the Turk rarely lost. And the great and good queued up to play it. The Turk beat Napoleon. It beat the great American thinker and diplomat Benjamin Franklin. It provided stiff opposition, albeit in defeat, to the Frenchman André Danican Philidor, thought then to be the world's best player. The writer Edgar Allan Poe watched the machine play in America in 1836 and speculated that there must be a human player inside its body. He was getting close, certainly closer than the many who believed the Turk was genuinely capable of thought.

The Turk was passed from one owner to the next, ending up neglected and forgotten in the back of a Philadelphia museum, where it was destroyed by fire in 1854. Three years later, Dr Silas Mitchell, the son of the machine's last owner, revealed its secret in the *Chess Monthly* magazine. 'There are no longer any reasons for concealing from the amateurs of chess the solution to this ancient enigma,' he said. 'No secret was ever kept as the Turk's has been. Guessed at, in part, many times, no one of the several explanations ever solved this amusing puzzle.'

SHOVE OFF
The Pub Game Bounder

There can be few greater bounders than a man who would cheat at shove ha'penny. But such a man turned up to the world championships of the traditional pub game, and was himself shoved out of the door when he was caught.

The game involves propelling coins, normally with the heel of the hand, up a slate lying flat on a table. The slate is lined horizontally. The idea is to get the coins to stop between the lines. To make it more fiendishly difficult, the slate is lubricated to make the coins travel faster.

In 1996, about 100 world title contenders converged on a pub in Leckhampton, Gloucestershire. Most were British, though three men flew in from Swaziland in southern Africa, where there is a thriving community of ha'penny shovers.

At stake was a gold cup and a £250 top prize and, with such riches on offer, it was probably inevitable that underhand tactics would be employed. Minutes before the event was due to begin, a referee saw a player from Devon wipe his hand across the slate. There is no worse transgression. Sweat makes the slate sticky, giving the player unfair control over his coins.

Tournament referee Jeff Bird said, 'I used our sweatometer, a machine that measures air humidity, and found out just what he was up to. I told him he was out of the competition.'

Roger Symms, the competition organiser, said, 'As soon as the Devon player was ordered off the slate, everyone else went out and washed and dried their hands.'

The cheat was heavily criticised by the 1995 world champion Tony Stevens, a 48-year-old Gloucestershire rat catcher, who was knocked out in the first round of his title defence. 'I have not practised enough,' he admitted. 'But I would never have dared wipe a sweaty hand across the slate.'

Chapter 8

Rotters

THE REFEREE'S A BANKER
Robert Hoyzer Shames the Bundesliga

Crooked referee Robert Hoyzer is a hate figure for Germans, and with good reason. The sneaky official's match-fixing antics dragged them through their biggest football scandal in decades just as they were about to host the World Cup.

Hoyzer – bleach-blond, perma-tanned and 6ft 5in – was a 25-year-old referee in the second division of the Bundesliga when the scam was exposed in early 2005. His extraordinary handling of a cup game between Paderborn and Bundesliga giants Hamburg the previous August had aroused the suspicions of four other refs, who alerted the German FA. Hoyzer had awarded underdogs Paderborn two highly dubious penalties, which helped them to a surprise 4-2 win, especially after he also sent off a Hamburg striker for protesting.

An investigation was launched and Hoyzer initially denied everything. But he eventually confessed he had taken bribes from a betting syndicate to award penalties and free kicks unfairly.

Within days, detectives had raided the homes of four Bundesliga refs and fourteen current or ex-players from Germany's second division. They also arrested Croatian brothers Milan, Filip and Ante Sapina who owned a Berlin sports café, the Café King, from where they ran their betting syndicate. Police found betting slips worth £1.6 million and a receipt for a new Ferrari. Another referee, Dominik Marks, was also arrested.

In court, Hoyzer admitted receiving £47,000 and a flat-screen TV from the brothers for fixing games. He said he was drunk when he first agreed to get involved, and his first attempt to fix a match backfired. Ante Sapina had bet on Paderborn having a half-time lead over Chemnitz FC in a league match – but it was 0-0 at half-time and Hoyzer had to refund his bribe.

A week later, he received £2,700 after unfairly awarding a penalty in a lower-league game, following which Sapina sent him a text message saying, 'Fatty, now you're my man!' The syndicate fixed at least 11 matches.

The prosecution recommended a suspended sentence for Hoyzer, since he had co-operated with the investigation so willingly and so usefully. The judge was having none of it. Keen to project a squeaky-clean image for Germany with the 2006 World Cup less than a year away, she locked him up for two years and five months, to his and everyone else's evident astonishment.

'A second division referee is well paid,' Judge Gerti Kramer told the Berlin District Court. 'He doesn't have to be good, but he must at least be neutral.'

The Sapina brothers were also jailed. Marks got a suspended sentence.

Interviewed by a German newspaper, Hoyzer described how he succumbed to temptation. 'I would party at Café King, drinking cocktails and Croatian schnapps. I would get through ten cocktails sometimes. One night, one of the brothers showed me a betting receipt with a €47,000 win. I thought, "Man, so much money!" He then asked, "Could we not do something here?" I drunkenly replied, "Of course, we could do everything."

'You do many things for money, things that you shouldn't do. I spent it all on fashionable clothes, partying and eating out. I didn't save any of it.'

ROBBED ROY
Judges' Terrible Blunder

Few could believe their eyes when boxing judges at the 1988 Seoul Olympics inexplicably handed gold to a South Korean local boy plainly beaten hands-down by the mighty American Roy Jones. The howls of protest were deafening.

Jones, from Pensacola, Florida, was a supreme talent. In the 1990s, he became arguably the world's best boxer, voted Fighter of the Decade by the Boxing Writers Association of America. But his defeat at Seoul, as an amateur light-middleweight, made headlines around the world. It remains one of the most outrageous judging decisions in Olympic history.

The atmosphere was intimidating and the officials were under considerable pressure as Jones, then 19, came up against South Korean Park Si-hun. Ten days earlier, a riot had broken out in the ring after a marginal decision went against another Korean. Bottles, glasses and chairs were thrown and the security chief detailed to protect the referee attacked him instead. The beaten Korean fighter demonstrated his displeasure at things not going his way by staging a 67-minute sit-down in the ring.

There could have been no such protest this time.

The fight wasn't even close; Jones simply overwhelmed Park Si-hun. During the three-round bout, he landed 86 punches to his opponent's 32. He seemed to pummel the Korean at will with his left hook. In the second round, he battered him so hard and so often that Park Si-hun was given a standing count of eight. Jones was just in a different class.

The fight ended and the judges from Hungary and the Soviet Union duly awarded Jones victory by a wide margin. Incredibly, their colleagues from Morocco, Uganda and Uruguay said the Korean had won by a whisker. Jones had lost 3-2. The South Korean had stolen his gold.

It was so grossly unfair that even some Koreans in the crowd joined in the booing. Heinz Birkle, a German leader of the AIBA, amateur boxing's governing body, said of the judges, 'I want to hit them in the face. It's criminal.' The AIBA immediately awarded Jones a special trophy as the tournament's outstanding boxer.

British judge Rod Robertson weighed in, branding the decision 'disgraceful'. Jones, in defeat, said simply, 'I am sick. So would anyone be who has been robbed.'

Years later, he revealed the following exchange with Park Si-hun: 'I went with an interpreter to face the guy I fought,' he said. 'I asked him, "Did

you win that fight?" He shook his head and said,
"No."'

Naturally, the South Koreans defended themselves and the judges. Seung-Youn Kim, head of
the country's amateur boxing association, said,
'The finals were fair. I cannot understand why
foreigners have a prejudice against Korea.'

The three errant judges were banned for two
years for incompetence. It took another eight
before the International Olympic Committee
appointed a commission to investigate in 1996. A
year later, it reported back. There was no evidence
of bribery – the decision stood; the gold belonged
to Park Si-hun, not Jones.

GOLDEN FLEECED
Soviet Scams at Moscow Olympics

No stone was left unturned to ensure the Soviet
Union won a stack of golds in front of the home
crowd at the Moscow Olympics of 1980. The
running of the javelin competition was particularly
suspect. One alleged ruse may be apocryphal. For
the other, there is more solid evidence.

The first ploy was ingenious. It has long been
said that every time a Soviet athlete was poised to
throw, the gates of the Lenin Stadium were

opened, allowing gusts of wind to propel the Soviet javelins a few extra metres and into the medal positions. Then the gates were closed again for non-Soviets. Whether this actually took place will probably never be known.

But the second ruse is more provable. The Soviet javelin-thrower, Dainis Kula, a 21-year-old Latvian, had scored foul throws on his first two attempts. He had to make the third count to qualify for the finals.

It was a decent effort, too, flying a good way, but it landed tail-first and bounced, failing to penetrate the field, as the rules say it must. And that should have been that – it was a no-throw. But the Soviet officials waved a flag to signal it was OK, ran out to measure it and announced it was 291ft 7in.

It was a stroke of luck for Kula, who went on to win gold. The Soviets took silver, too, and narrowly missed out on bronze.

Chapter 9

Sneaks

UNDERHAND TACTICS
Greg Chappell and the Grubber

When two Prime Ministers – including your own –
condemn your deviousness, it's a good clue that
you may have gone over the top.

Greg Chappell has had to live with the disgrace
of his ultimate act of gamesmanship for the best
part of three decades. Chappell was part of a
ruthless Aussie cricket team in the 1970s and early
1980s. But even his team-mates were dismayed by
the literally underhand tactics the skipper used to
prevent New Zealand from tieing a one-day
international in February 1981.

The Kiwis needed a six off the last ball – admittedly the tallest of tall orders, especially given that the batsman, Brian McKechnie, was a number ten who had only just arrived at the crease. McKechnie was a strong bloke – and a rugby All Black – but even he would struggle to clear the boundary of the huge Melbourne Cricket Ground.

Chappell, however, was leaving nothing to chance. He strolled up to his younger brother Trevor, bowling the final over, and ordered him to bowl a 'grubber' – that is, to roll the ball bowls-style along the ground, making it almost impossible to hit in the air. Even the Aussie wicketkeeper Rod Marsh, not known for giving opponents an inch, shook his head and waved his arms hoping to dissuade the younger Chappell from such a sneaky course.

But Trevor did as he was told, trundling the ball the 22 yards to McKechnie, who played a faintly comical forward-defensive shot to block it. No run. New Zealand had lost.

McKechnie threw his bat to the ground in fury. Bruce Edgar, the batsman at the other end, flicked a V-sign at the bowler, and the Kiwi captain Geoff Howarth ran down from the pavilion to complain to the umpires.

His protests were in vain. Incredibly, the grubber

was at that time not against the rules. While Chappell Sr was guilty of gamesmanship on a grand scale, he had not cheated. 'If it's written in the rules of the game, it is fair play,' he said later.

Others disagreed. New Zealand's Prime Minister Robert Muldoon called it 'the most disgusting incident I can recall in the history of cricket... an act of true cowardice'. His Aussie counterpart Malcolm Fraser had to admit it ran 'contrary to the traditions of the game'.

Even Greg's older brother Ian Chappell, a man known for his own merciless captaincy of Australia, asked, 'How low can you go?'

Twenty years later, Chappell came clean about that infamous decision. He said it was a 'cry for help' and that he was 'mentally unfit' to captain the side that day because he was exhausted by a relentless schedule of Test matches and one-day internationals. 'I was exhausted... I was fed up,' he said. 'The under-arm had very little to do with winning that game of cricket because, in fact, we'd won the game. They weren't going to get six off the last ball. It was my statement. My cry for help was, "You're not listening, this might help you sit up and take notice."

'If they told me I'd never play again I wouldn't have cared, which gives an indication of the state of mind I was in. As I walked off the ground, I was in shock. I had no feelings at all. But then a young girl ran across in front of me, stopped and tugged on the sleeve of my shirt. She looked at me and said, "You cheated."

'I had known it wasn't going to be well received, but it was only then I realised that maybe it was going to be worse than I thought.'

Bowler Trevor said, 'Greg copped a lot of flak from people in Australian cricket. Probably everyone in New Zealand was upset. Robert Muldoon thought it was fitting that the Australian cricket team were wearing canary yellow.'

McKechnie's anger subsided quickly. 'I was disgusted at the time,' he says. 'But an hour after the game, we were just sort of joking about it.' And he is satisfied with Greg's explanation as to his motives. 'He was under pressure during the game and wanted to leave the field. He stood at long-off, near the boundary. That's unusual for a captain. I've only spoken to him once since, and we never spoke about that. It was just one of those unfortunate things. But I wish it had never happened to me. Everywhere I go in New Zealand, you can bet your life someone will ask me a question about it.'

It won't happen to another batsman, either. After the Chappell fiasco, the grubber was quickly outlawed.

UNHOLEY STINK
Golf Cheat David Robertson

Golf is one of the 'cleanest' sports there is, mainly because the punishments for transgressors are swift and brutal. David Robertson, once one of the world's most promising young players, felt the full force of that justice when he was rumbled for systematic and blatant cheating.

A butcher's son from Dunbar, Scotland, Robertson was a teenage prodigy, a British Youths champion who played for Scotland at full international level aged just 14. In 1972, at just 15, he qualified for the Open, one of the youngest players ever to do so. But his career effectively ended during the final qualifying round for the 1985 Open in Deal, Kent.

Robertson's deception worked like this – he would drive his ball off the tee and march down to the green, ensuring he arrived before his playing partners. Then he would bend down and apparently place his marker where the ball landed. Except Robertson was not leaving his marker where the ball stopped at all. Instead, he was picking up the ball, carrying the marker on his putter and ambling towards the hole before surreptitiously dropping the marker in a better spot. He hoped that when his opponents arrived they would be none the wiser – they would merely see his marker, impressively near the hole.

But Robertson lacked subtlety. He wasn't content to shift the ball a few inches to a slightly better lie. He was moving it up to 20 feet at a time, and was spotted by at least half-a-dozen witnesses. Among them was his caddie, who threw down his bag in disgust after ten holes and walked off.

After 14 holes, Robertson's playing partners reported him to an official. Championship bosses heard the evidence and disqualified him. His offence – in official parlance – was 'not replacing his ball in the correct position on the green'.

It emerged that the 28-year-old player had been reported for similar offences before. And he was then handed the most severe punishment in golfing history – a 20-year ban from playing as a pro on the PGA European Tour and a £20,000 fine.

Ken Schofield, head of the PGA European Tour, said, 'It's a very sad day for the tour and for golf. Equally, the findings indicate the degree the tour will go to protect itself, and it is a warning to anyone down the years. The great majority play the game the way it is intended to be. The tour's intention is to keep it that way.

'The tournament committee took into account Mr Robertson's past record. There was then evidence from six witnesses – four caddies and

Mr Robertson's two playing partners. Mr Robertson had two caddies because one retired at the tenth hole.'

At an appeal hearing a few months later, the punishment got worse. Robertson was banned for life from the PGA European Tour, though the fine was scrapped. Seven years later, golf's authorities finally showed Robertson some mercy and gave him back his amateur status, allowing him to play in amateur tournaments in Scotland, but his dream of a professional career was over.

Robertson always maintained he was innocent and, more than a decade on from the 1985 Open, was still bitter about his punishment. 'I could have robbed a bank and got less of a sentence,' he said.

ADMISSION OF DEFEET
Ffyona Campbell

Ffyona Campbell was the first woman to walk around the world. At least, that's what everyone believed for two years – until she confessed she did part of her trek in a van.

Campbell's apparently astonishing feat – a walk of 19,586 miles achieved over 11 years – made worldwide headlines when she finally finished at John O'Groats, Scotland, in October 1994.

She had started off from there aged 16 in 1983, walking to Land's End in Cornwall. Two years later, she walked across America, from New York to Los Angeles; then Australia, from Sydney to Perth; the length of Africa from Cape Town to Tangiers; and across Europe from Algeciras, Spain, to Dover. From there, she walked back to Scotland.

Tears streamed down Campbell's face as a crowd of relatives and well-wishers greeted her. She entered the *Guinness Book of Records* as the first woman – and only the fourth person – to complete the trip, crossing four continents at up to 30 miles a day and wearing out 100 pairs of shoes.

'I'm sorry it has ended,' she said. 'At the end of every other leg of the journey, I rushed into the sea and said, "Thank God it's over." It hasn't been like that this time.'

Her dad, a former Royal Marine, gave her his coveted green beret, awarded for endurance. 'You've earned it,' he told her, suspecting nothing.

Campbell, then 27, said she'd always had a restless spirit due to moving home 24 times before she was 16. 'I need to exercise every day. I get really depressed if I don't. Walking's a tremendous way to keep fit,' she explained.

The initial plan, she went on, was just to walk from John O'Groats to Land's End 'to sort my life out'. But the idea expanded – and then sponsors came on board. 'This has been a piece of history shared by a lot of people,' she said. 'I've just gone out there and done my best.'

And that was how it stayed for two years, until Campbell made an astonishing confession in a book about her great adventure – she had cheated. During the epic leg across the US, she had secretly become pregnant by one of the back-up drivers who accompanied her in a van full of equipment and food. As the pregnancy progressed, she found it impossible to keep up the punishing schedule of 23 miles a day. Finally, for several weeks, and over a stretch of about 1,000 miles, she jumped in the van for regular lifts.

Campbell revealed that she kept quiet about the dodge to avoid letting the sponsors down. She resumed walking full-time only after having an abortion in New Mexico. Consumed by guilt, she took drugs, including heroin, and considered suicide.

In her confession, she asked to be removed from the record books. 'I shouldn't be remembered as the first woman to walk around the world,' she said. 'I leave that accolade for another. When I cheated, I broke the unwritten rule of the *Guinness Book Of Records*. People were walking beside me as a role model, they were respecting me. To them, I owe my biggest apology.'

Campbell claimed that a year after completing her trek in 1994, she returned to America to walk the 1,000-mile stretch she skipped first time around. But it was too late. Her achievement was fatally flawed.

Her mother Angela said Campbell had confessed to her before the book came out. 'She confided in me, as daughters do in their mothers,' she said. 'It was a big shock at first, and hard to come to terms with, but she had a very good reason.'

Chapter 10

A Cheat? Not Me!

DIRT IN THE POCKET
Michael Atherton's Terrible Week

Ball tampering has long been an explosive issue in cricket. In the years before Hansie Cronje raised cheating to a new level, there was no worse crime.

Michael Atherton was England captain and an opening batsman of true grit. The infamous 'dirt in the pocket' affair that engulfed him for ten days in the summer of 1994 remains the one blemish on a magnificent career. Even though he has always made a convincing case that he never broke the rules, the storm of controversy that erupted was immense.

The main point of altering a cricket ball's

condition is to exaggerate its movement in the air or off the pitch, thus to bamboozle the batsman. Under the rules, it can be polished, dried with a towel or have mud removed from it, but that's it. It cannot be roughened by rubbing on the ground or gouged with a fingernail. Its seam must not be picked, or raised in any other way.

On Saturday, 23 July 1994, England were on the receiving end of a drubbing from a buoyant South African side making their first appearance at Lords, the home of cricket, since being plunged into sporting exile in the 1960s over apartheid. England were fielding in stifling humidity when, shortly before the tea interval, TV cameras showed Atherton – the young Lancastrian who was made captain at 25 the previous year – repeatedly reaching into his pocket, then withdrawing his hand and seemingly rubbing something into the ball.

It was not clear exactly what he was up to, but the Australian match referee Peter Burge was sure as hell going to find out. When Atherton came in for tea, the England manager Keith Fletcher and chairman of selectors Ray Illingworth demanded an explanation. Atherton told them the story he maintains to this day – the bowler Darren Gough needed one side of the ball kept rough and dry to aid his swing bowling. Atherton scooped some dirt from a disused pitch into his pocket and used it several times to dry his hands and the ball – which was becoming moist in the humidity. This was enough to satisfy Fletcher and Illingworth – but Burge wanted to hear it first-hand.

When play ended, the England captain was summoned to the referee's room with Fletcher and the match umpires. Burge asked the umpires if the ball's condition had been changed and they said no. He then asked Atherton what he'd been doing and whether he had an artificial substance in his pocket.

Burge, once a hard-hitting Aussie batsman, was an intimidating figure and Atherton a rabbit in his headlights. He told Burge he had merely been drying his hands in his pockets. Convincing himself that dirt was not the artificial substance to which Burge referred, he declined to mention it. It was a ghastly mistake.

As Atherton said in his autobiography years later, 'Burge looked fearsome, stern and headmasterly in his office that evening. In short, I panicked. I sensed that he felt I was guilty and I was not about to incriminate myself.'

Atherton went to bed that night unaware of the ferocity of the media storm he was about to endure for the next week. The problem was that the sanitised version of events he gave Burge did not tally with his explanation to Fletcher and Illingworth, which spelled out that he was using dirt to maintain, albeit not to alter, the ball's condition.

When Burge found out about this discrepancy, he hit the roof. The next day, after England lost the match, he told Atherton he would have suspended him for the next two Tests, probably costing him the captaincy, had he known about the dirt. Illingworth agreed to fine him heavily, both for using the dirt and for lying to the referee.

A disastrous press conference ensued which was somehow broadcast live on TV without anyone in the room knowing. Atherton's unlikely interrogator-in-chief was Jonathan Agnew, the genial BBC cricket correspondent and popular *Test Match Special* radio commentator. A famous picture shows Agnew's gangling figure almost clambering over a disconsolate and furious Atherton to grill Illingworth, sitting alongside him.

Atherton was front-page news for a week, with all manner of commentators – in the news and sports pages – circling him like sharks scenting blood. Pundits from Agnew to Test legend Geoff Boycott insisted he had to go.

It was not so much the use of dirt as the lying that had done the damage. An editorial in the *Times* read, 'If the captain of England's cricket team fails to uphold the values of his society or the values to which his society aspires, he is unworthy of that uncommon honour which the captaincy represents. He should be replaced.'

Atherton almost buckled, considering long and hard whether he should quit. But in keeping with the stubbornness that was the essence of his batting, he stayed on, reasoning that he hadn't cheated on the field, even if he had not told the match referee the whole truth.

It was not long before his talent won back his popular support. Under intense pressure and scrutiny in the next Test, he made a gritty 99 and was cheered to the rafters as he walked back to the pavilion.

It is a testament to his career that such a huge scandal is now a mere footnote to it. Atherton was the backbone of a generally failing England team up to his retirement in 2001 and received a standing ovation at the Oval on leaving the field after his last Test innings – during which he scored just 9.

Now a TV commentator of considerable skill, Atherton says this of the incident: 'It all seems to me to have been a storm in a teacup, although that is, of course, for others to judge.' But he does concede, 'You can be judged by how you react in the most difficult times... and I failed myself then.'

TOILETGATE
The Chess Rivals' Dirty War

A cheating scandal dubbed 'Toiletgate' threatened to flush the 2006 World Chess Championship down the pan. Not that there was anything untoward about the manner in which Russian Vladimir Kramnik arrived at each move. But his Bulgarian opponent Veselin Topalov was convinced there was... and that Kramnik's loo was the focal point of foul play.

There is precious little trust between officials and players at the highest level of the ancient game. CCTV monitors the playing area as well as the rest areas where the combatants relax while waiting for each other to move. Each player is frisked by an electronic scanner before every game. The one place not covered by Big Brother is the private toilet each player has behind him.

With 31-year-old Kramnik leading the 12-game series 3-2, his opponent's manager made an astonishing complaint – that the Russian Grandmaster was using his toilet fifty times per game... and that it was suspicious. The suggestion was that one of the world's élite players was retreating to the loo to consult a chess computer over his next move.

The timing was unfortunate for Kramnik. The

president of the International Chess Federation, Kirsan Ilyumzhinov, was away from the match at Elista, in the Russian republic of Kalmykia, for a summit with President Vladimir Putin. In his absence, a committee of officials sided with the Bulgarian immediately. Without even discussing the matter with Kramnik, they ruled that the players must now share a single toilet.

Kramnik's loo was shut and locked, to his outrage. The Russian insisted he simply liked to walk around as his opponent pondered. Visiting the toilet gave him more space to roam than if he confined himself to his tiny rest area. Plus, he said, he had chronic arthritis which made him urinate more than normal.

Then he produced his own conspiracy theory: The officials on the committee who closed down his loo were mates of Topalov and biased in his favour. He demanded the immediate reinstatement of his toilet. But it remained closed.

In protest, Kramnik sat out the next game, refusing to budge from his rest area, and forfeited the result when time ran out.

Some level of sanity was restored with the return of Ilyumzhinov from his Putin summit. He reinstated Kramnik's toilet rights and the match proceeded, but not without further controversy, this time from Kramnik's manager, who claimed the Bulgarians were secretly plotting to install a surveillance microchip in Kramnik's convenience.

In the end, Toiletgate seemed to strengthen Kramnik's play. Chess experts said the stress somehow made him even more wary and analytical than usual. It paid dividends – Kramnik won the match and the $1 million world championship.

BODYLINE
Cricket's Greatest Crisis

Whether 'Bodyline', the aggressive bowling tactic with which England won the Ashes in 1932–33, can be called cheating depends entirely on whether you are Australian. England fans correctly argue that it was within the rules. To them, it was a masterful ploy decades ahead of its time. Some Aussies, hardened by their modern team's own ruthlessness, believe this, too. But there is still a hardcore of Australian fans bitter about Bodyline three-quarters of a century on.

Compared with the non-stop aggression of modern Test cricket, the tactic seems small beer. But in the 1930s, it represented an assault on the gentlemanly spirit in which the game was then played. It remains cricket's greatest cheating controversy because it transcended the sport and threatened diplomatic and economic relations between England and Australia.

Bodyline involved bowling very fast, short-pitched balls on the batsman's leg side, which would rear up and threaten to hit him. The idea was to lure the batsman into raising his bat to defend himself against injury, resulting in a deflection that could be caught by a pack of fielders placed near him on the leg side.

The technique was devised mainly to counter the Australian genius Don Bradman, still considered the finest batsman in history, but perceived then as weaker against short-pitched, fast bowling.

When Australia won the Ashes in England in 1930, Bradman averaged 139 runs per innings. He was unstoppable. After that defeat, England's Oxford-educated captain Douglas Jardine summoned the fast bowlers Harold Larwood and Bill Voce to the restaurant of a London hotel to discuss a new tactic, known then as 'fast leg theory'. Larwood and Voce agreed it might work against Bradman and, for the next two seasons, practised it with great success for their home county, Nottinghamshire.

An outraged Australian public first encountered it during the opening tour match when England went Down Under hoping to regain the Ashes in the winter of 1932/33. Cricket was a gentler game then. There were no helmets, and padding was far less substantial than it is now. One by one, batsmen from an Australian XI were left battered and bruised. The risk of 'fast leg theory' causing very serious injury seemed considerable. Worse still for the home crowds, it seemed to dry up their team's runs.

An Aussie journalist wired his newspaper a report on England's new bowling tactic, abbreviating his own phrase 'in the line of the body' to 'bodyline' to cut the cost of the telegram. Thus the infamous phrase was born.

Australian newspapers claimed a batsman would be killed. English papers retaliated by calling the Aussies bad losers and 'squealers', an opinion the public shared. But this was long before anyone could watch matches on TV – no one in England could see how aggressively Jardine was getting Larwood and Voce to bowl. Even some of England's players were troubled by Bodyline. One fast bowler refused to be involved.

But the ploy worked. The Australian batting suffered, ironically with the exception of Bradman. He was hit by the ball only once, and got round Bodyline by moving to the leg side to hit the ball through the vacant field on the off-side. It worked to an extent, and he ended the series with a terrific average of nearly 57 per innings – although this was way down on his career average and his average during the previous Ashes series.

The controversy peaked with a near-riot during an infamous Third Test at Adelaide. Larwood fractured the Australian wicket-keeper's skull and felled their captain Bill Woodfull with a blow above the heart, though neither using Bodyline. Jardine then rubbed salt in Aussie wounds by shifting his fielders into Bodyline catching positions immediately after Woodfull's injury. The crowd went berserk and police had to move in to protect England's players.

Woodfull later told England's tour manager Pelham Warner, 'There are two teams out there. One is playing cricket. The other is making no attempt to do so.' The Australian Board of Control for Cricket cabled England's cricket chiefs, the MCC, in London, saying, 'Bodyline bowling assumed such proportions as to menace best interests of game, making protection of body by batsmen the main consideration. Causing intensely bitter feeling between players as well as injury. In our opinion is unsportsmanlike. Unless stopped at once likely to upset friendly relations existing between Australia and England.'

The MCC and the British public were outraged

at being branded 'unsportsmanlike' and demanded a retraction.

It was 30 January 1933 – the day Adolf Hitler came to power in Germany – but there was only one story obsessing England and Australia – the cricket. The Aussies hit back at the MCC, sending another telegram of complaint which sneered, 'We appreciate your difficulty in dealing with the matter without having seen the actual play.'

England threatened to scrap the Fourth and Fifth Tests unless the slur was withdrawn – and an international incident was in full cry. The British and Australian publics were at loggerheads, each boycotting the other's produce. Diplomats were called in, fearing the crisis could severely damage trade between the two countries. Finally, Australian Prime Minister Joseph Lyons warned his cricket board of the dire economic consequences of a boycott of Aussie goods in Britain – and the board backed down. They withdrew the slur and the remaining Tests went ahead, England winning the series 4-1.

English crowds only began to have reservations about Bodyline when they finally saw it first-hand in the summer of 1933. Larwood and Voce used it to good effect for Nottinghamshire and English skipper Jardine had to face it himself when the touring West Indians adopted it. England's opening batsman Wally Hammond was hit on the chin by one Bodyline ball.

It was clear Bodyline was damaging the game. Within two years, a new law gave umpires the duty to prevent bowlers from aiming at the batsman with intent to cause injury. A later law limited the number of fielders who could be placed behind the batsman on the leg side, negating Bodyline still further.

England's relations with Australia remained strained throughout the 1930s as a result of the controversy. English immigrants Down Under were targets of abuse, as were Aussies in England.

The war to defeat Hitler's Nazis and their Japanese allies reunited the nations in the 1940s. But Bodyline still has the power to raise hackles whenever cricket fans from the two countries meet.